Painted
by *Words*

By LaurieL

Copyright © 2022 **Lauretta Groom Publishing**

All rights reserved. No part of this publication may be reproduced, distributed, or transmitted in any form or by any means, including photocopying, recording, or other electronic or mechanical methods, without the prior written permission of the publisher, except in the case of brief quotations embodied in critical reviews and certain other noncommercial uses permitted by copyright law. For permission requests, write to the publisher, addressed "Attention: Book Rights and Permission," at the address below.

Published in the United States of America

ISBN 978-1-959173-29-8 (SC)

Lauretta Groom Publishing
222 West 6th Street
Suite 400, San Pedro, CA, 90731
25wisvol@live.com.

Ordering Information and Rights Permission:

Quantity sales. Special discounts might be available on quantity purchases by corporations, associations, and others. For details, contact the publisher at the address above.

For Book Rights Adaptation and other Rights Permission. Call us at toll-free 1-888-945-8513 or send us an email at admin@stellarliteray.com.

Table of Contents

Chapter 1 1
Chapter 2 17
Chapter 3 29
Chapter 4 38
Chapter 5 67
Chapter 6 77
Chapter 7 94
Chapter 8 115
Chapter 9 135
Chapter 10 149
Chapter 11 180
Chapter 12 213
Chapter 13 223
Chapter 14 243
Chapter 15 262
Chapter 16 283
Conclusion 290

The Love of a Soldier

I'm an old soldier; I have no shame. Fighting and killing is how I was trained.
If you are in need, I'll be there indeed so, don't look down your nose at me.
I'll protect them all and train them to fight;
Don't turn your back on me because you think I'm not right.
For when you're in need-Because a of Dictators' rule,
I'll be the soldier to take him to school.
So, no matter how much you hate me for what I do,
I'll always be willing to put my life on the line for you!

Written By Mark J. Groom

This book is dedicated to
Mark J. Groom

To my beloved husband Mark.
Without you, there would have
Been no story to write about.
You are my life, my strength, my love.
Thank you so much for being there.
I love you very much!

Chapter 1

Some say there is a day in everyone's life that changes it forever. Events happen that seems really small at the time, but after a while, its effect on your life is huge. Usually, it's something that when it happens, you barely notice it. It's enough that you remember it, but you don't give it much thought at the time. After it happens, you go on with whatever it is your doing. Then one day, the effects of this event hit you like a train.

Thinking back, I never really believed this could be true until after it actually happened to me. It was a while after wards when I realized it even took place. In quiet times late at night I would think about old memories and play back events and do the "what if" game. I would realize during these moments, what happened and why. This is something I still do today. As I reflect on events, I am amazed how things always works out. Often, I would find myself thinking, how could something so small have such a big effect on my whole life?

See, I grew up in a small town where it didn't really matter what you were inside, what you believed or even what you stood for. What seemed to matter to everyone in my town was what your last name was and how big the dollar sign attached to it is. Unless your family was rich or had the right name, you really were not seen as important or paid much attention to. I remember well how in school the teachers tried not to show such favoritism, but it was still pretty easy to see who their pets were.

Maybe because I felt I was not favored, it was easier for me to see, but I saw it just the same. The "in" kids never seemed to have a finger pointed at them whenever there was trouble. After a scuffle on the playground, the teacher usually believed the "in" child over anyone else. Not that there were a lot of fights or anything like that, but there was the occasional tiff or argument. Not all events were handled by the teachers. We did on occasion solve our own problems.

I remember one event. At least I remember the bits and pieces of what happened. It all falls together when I heard both sides at a much later time, but as I look back, it was a very significant event in my life. It was a day just like every other day. It happened during recess.

There I was standing on the playground which was paved in blacktop. It was a normal run of the mill playground. It had monkey bars, climbing gyms, and two sets of swings that everyone ran for when the bell rang and a couple of slides. There were some squares painted for playing hopscotch and there were a couple of basketball hoops located at the end. The majority of the rest of the area was wide open where kids usually played football. Why they didn't play football on the grass was always beyond me.

Sometimes we were not allowed to play on the

grass due to the time of year and the wetness. But if it were me, I wouldn't want to get tackled on the blacktop any time of year. I was standing just a few feet away from the slides and monkey bars when it happened. My friends and I were throwing a ball back and forth I believe. This part is a little fuzzy because it was such a long time ago, but I do remember we were involved in a pretty good game. I was not really paying much attention to what other kids were doing around us. I guess I really should have been, but at the time, I didn't see the need.

I remember I was smiling and laughing when it happened. Out of the blue, some kid barreled into me knocking me flat on my backside. The hit was pretty good because I remember it was a little hard to get my next couple of breaths. It knocked the wind clean out of me. I just remember sitting there wondering what in the heck had just happened. There was someone asking me if I was alright and a hand was helping me get up on my feet. I pretty much got up, brushed off my pants, said "Uh huh." and went back to my friends who were watching me with their mouths wide open.

I don't recall much of what happened after that, but after talking about it with the guy who "ran" me over, it all makes sense now. Apparently, there was a pretty good football game going on. A long pass was being thrown and there was a boy who was running to catch it. He has his eye on the ball and nothing else. After making a stupendous catch, he turned to run to make the touchdown when he plows right into this dumb old girl who was standing there in his way. The boy really didn't mean to hurt the girl and he knew he hit her hard. He felt bad as he helped her up wanting to be sure she was okay. He was amazed at the time that she didn't cry or complain. All he could see were her bright blue eyes, and think wow, look at how pretty they are.

He said he felt so bad when he grabbed her hand to help her up. As he watched her walk back to her friends, her older sister popped out of the woodwork and chewed on him for hurting her little sister. He became angry because she acted like he tried to hurt the girl on purpose. She was in his face yelling at him, so he yelled back. He told her to get out of his face and how could such a cute little girl have such an ugly older sister! I don't remember that part, but I do remember the fear the event instilled in me.

From that point on, whenever anyone played football around me, I had the most over bearing fear someone was going to run me over. If a game started up, I usually headed well away from it. When I had to walk through where some kids were playing, I had to run to get out of the way even if I wasn't in the way. I never knew why I felt this way until after that memory was relived and remembered.

Thinking back, that day was one of those days that affected the rest of my life. That boy, the one that ran me over told me after that fateful day, he always noticed me no matter where he was or where I was. He said my blue eyes and beautiful smile was what he loved to watch. I guess maybe events that take place affect more than one person. Maybe no one really knows what the total effect on life these events have. I guess life's path is pretty unforeseeable and inconceivable at the time, but after pondering on it for a while, a person can really understand and see how things work out.

The town I grew up in was pretty much, what I'd call boring. Nothing exciting ever happened. There was nothing cool to do or nowhere to go to have fun or hang out with your friends unless you planned to meet at the park or the swimming pool. These places were really only usable in the summer months. The rest of the time you could go there, but the pool was closed during school months. Unless it was warm enough, you really didn't want to be standing anywhere outside in the cold.

The town was blessed with more than its share of churches and bars. We had every religion covered except for maybe Jewish or Muslim. These seemed segregated too. People each thought theirs was better and they were stuck in their own religious clicks, but to me it never mattered. I figured it all went to the same God, so why did it matter how it got there.

In our church, we actually had 2 churches. Back in the day, the older one for on south side of town and a newer one on the north side. The south side was for the Italians and the lower-class working families and anyone who lived on the south side. The north side was for the upper classes and anyone living in that area. By the time I was there, I don't think anyone thought of the classes of people anymore. They just went to the church they liked or if it was closer to their homes.

As far as bars, taverns or saloons whatever you prefer to call them, they were located all up and down our main street. It seemed like in every other building up or down the street was a bar. These places were not for children unless they went there with their folks. If they did, they usually got to play video games, drink pop and eat chips as long as they did it quiet like and didn't bother anyone. The bars were not a place a kid could go to have real fun and just be a kid.

Come to think of it, there was only one time a "bar" was a kid's hang out when I was young. It used to be a biker bar, but my friend's folks bought it and turned it into a kid's hang out. They had a pool table, video games, pop, and tap beer for the adults and a grill for short order food. I was never there after 11:00 pm because that was my curfew on the weekends. I heard it would get a bit more exciting the later it was, but when I was there, it was normally pretty quiet. I would play a few video games, but would play more pool than anything because you could make a game last. I knew most of the people that hung out and we all got along pretty good.

Every now and then, someone from another town would come in and change things up for a bit, but all in all, it was pretty quiet. I would get bored sometimes, but like I said, I mostly practiced my pool game. My favorite game was called Slop. It all had to do with attitude. You aimed at a ball and didn't have to call which one you meant. All you had to do was act like you meant for which ever ball that went in even if it wasn't the one you were aiming at. As long as one of your balls went in, it was cool and you got to shoot again. The only ball you had to call was the eight ball.

After a while, I started to get good. Not competition good, but good enough to be comfortable to play no matter who is watching. I would even impress folks when I'd get that shot you can't hit unless you are left-handed or unless you can reach clear across the table. Since I was vertically challenged, reaching across the table was not an option. I would shoot it behind my back and most times I could make it. Of course, that was before the middle age spread hit me. I did try that move a time or two recently and I still am not too bad at it. At least I could still reach the ball with that awkward shot.

Yes, the town I lived in was a place where you would sit and literally watch the world go by. News would come and go of something famous or exciting happening but it normally was always happening in some other town or some other faraway place. Folks would talk about it like it was sure special and there was no other event that was happening that could quite come as close to the importance of it. As exciting as it was to hear of such things, it was almost aggravating because that's all folks would talk about. You'd feel like if you heard that story one more time, your head was going to blow up.

When folks got a hold of a story, it was like a dog getting a hold of a bone. They would never forget and never let go. Sometimes they'd even add their own accounting to spice things up. So, depending on who was doing the telling, you could get various versions. I guess maybe that's how legends get started. Stories told over and over and spiced up a mite here and there to make things more interesting. After a while, who knows if it is true or not or if the story was factual or fictional. Long as it sounds good, folks are happy with the telling and as long as no one is hurt, what is the harm? Sometimes someone is always hurt.

We had a pretty wide variety of folks in our town. I don't think it was different than any other town. We had our upstanding folk, normal folk, heroes, wannabe actors and actress', artists, thieves, druggies, and drunks. I guess a person can't expect no different with all those bars huh? Like in most small towns, there are the folks that think they own it. Don't forget about the ones who have a need to know everyone's business and can only find shame in what they find out.

We have a major grape vine and certain folks run it. There were people you could tell something to and before the day was out, the whole town would know about it. You all know the type I'm talking of; the kind that live for gossip. This is the kind of person that doesn't care if they are hearing or spreading the truth or not. The juicier the information, the more excited they'd get. You could tell they were just itching to get somewhere where they could start spreading the new info they just got. It didn't matter if it really happened or not, if it is not wild enough to suit them, they embellish on the story just to spice it up.

Then there was the type of people who was the kind that likes to judge folks. After hearing something, true or not, they look at you and no matter what you do, think or act, they always find fault. There is no way you can ever make up for what you did or what they think you did. They would look down their nose and shake their head. You just knew what they were thinking and you knew you were done for in their book. The type of folks that I really have no time for were the ones that are loud mouthed, mean and violent.

These guys always know how to do everything and how to handle every situation. You all know this kind. This loud mouth braggart always spouts off with how things happened to them, worse than anything had ever happened to anyone else. No matter how bad someone had things, way worse has happened to them. As they handled it 100 times better than anyone one else did.

Yea, I know if you really think about it, you know someone who fits in each of these categories. Don't get me wrong, there are some mighty fine folks as well mixed in with the bad. If it weren't for these wonderful people, you'd always want to carry around some kind of weapon and take care of the whole mess. Now, don't go thinking I'm a violent person. I'm not, but it's just some folks brings out the bad in me just as some folks bring out the good as well. I just want to know why the bad always seem to run across my path and why there just seems to be so many of them.

Maybe it's just my time to be sheer mean and ornery, but in my life, I believe I've had my fill of those types of people. I guess maybe they are there so the good do really stand out and makes you think about the things you do to others. Maybe, just maybe life is not meant to be lived in a way that we sleep through it and not notice things. Maybe the whole thing is just a learning experience we are supposed to remember and grow from. I guess school never really is over then, is it.

Speaking of school, I remember, we had our clicks there too. If you don't know what a click is, that's okay. I'll try to explain things as I go. Not knowing what things mean is not a bad thing. It's when you don't know about something and you don't ask any questions to help you understand about it, that's bad. Like I always say, there is no such thing as a stupid question. But then again, this can be pushed in certain situations, but for the most part it is true.

A click is slang for a class or group of people or things with the same characteristics. One of my grandma's sayings was "Birds of a feather flock together". I've heard so many sayings in my life; it just comes natural for them to pop in my head at opportune times. You get the idea. Anyway, the first group or click was the kids who had the "right" last name and who had everything cool.

Anything that was new and expensive, they had it given to them on a silver platter. They had designer clothes, all the cool gadgets, and expensive shoes and coats. They only talked to you if they were bragging of what they had or making fun of what little you had. Like I said before, these kids had the "right" last name. Their parents were very well off, had great jobs and didn't have any money problems. They considered themselves to be right important and very upper class.

In my eyes, this was a status that never mattered to me because I saw what was really on the inside and the two sure didn't match. These kids usually did what they wanted and didn't worry about the consequences. They knew they could get out of any trouble by claiming to be the angel folks thought them to be. This rankled me because I never thought that was fair. I figured if you don't want trouble, don't start trouble. You shouldn't be able to make trouble without the worry of the repercussions. It's like going out and breaking laws without worrying if the cops are going to come and arrest you. It was the same difference in my book. I could never understand how they always got away with it.

Then there were the kids who were just a step below them. These kids had a lot too, but they weren't as vocal about it. Their parents were also pretty well off, but didn't think they were as high and mighty. These kids talked to the uppers as well as to the lowers. That's because they were usually cousins to the uppers and friends to the lowers. They were pretty decent and didn't cause much trouble. If one was your friend, you are kind of worried about what was going to happen during a conflict. There was the worry of which side they'd be on. There is another saying, "Blood is thicker than water". Remember the cousin thing. They were decent enough but when the chips were down, you really needed to know who was on your side and who was not. It's like walking a fine line. You didn't want to fall or get pushed by someone you thought was a trusted friend.

The third click was the lower-class kids. These kids were the ones whose parents were either split or else they just didn't have the high paying jobs the uppers had. The working-class stiffs is the term I remember hearing when I was little. These were the scapegoats. If there was any trouble, they usually got blamed and of course they were not the teacher's pets, so they ended up taking the brunt of whatever was happening. It didn't make them bad or anything, just not looked upon in a good light at times.

Then of course there came the kids that were even down more than the lowers. These were the kids that just didn't seem to fit in with any click. They were made of up the kids who had mental problems, learning disorders, or were just plain social outcasts because of being violent, mean or into illegal actives. These kids always seemed to band together and were picked on the worst. I always felt sorry for these kids unless of course if they were mean or doing illegal things.

There were times when I tried to protect or help them. Not that I felt I was better than they were; I just figured they didn't deserve to be treated that way. It wasn't right in my book, not that I wanted a pat on the back. I just didn't believe it was right. So, where I could, I did something and where I couldn't, I still did what I could. I didn't get into any fights or anything, but if you hollered at the right time, "Hey, quit that or hey, leave that kid alone.", you could get someone's attention that would stop it. And you'd be surprised at what a loud word and a mean look will do at the right time. Not that I was some hero on a white horse, but at least I could sleep at night knowing I did something to try to stop a wrong.

I guess the first time I really noticed there was a difference in the way kids was treated was at a school Halloween Party one year. One of our family's pastimes was to watch the Carol Burnett show on TV. Mom would pop a huge bowl of popcorn and we'd sit there eating popcorn, drinking pop and watch the show. My grandma never cared to watch as she said she couldn't see it anyway, so she'd sit out in the kitchen by the heat register. She would cover up with a lap blanket and eat her popcorn. Every now and then, you'd hear her tell Mom how good the popcorn was and she didn't know how mom made it so good. She didn't have good teeth and mom could never figure out how she could eat that corn and not much else without complaining she just couldn't chew it.

Anyway, I just loved to watch the comedian, Tim Conway. I remember one episode that showed him with an extra pair of legs. It cracked me up. For Halloween that year, I wanted to make my own costume. Since I promised mom, I'd use old clothes in the attic, she let me do what I wanted. I took an old pair of pants and cut the seam around the crotch and the backside, leaving the two legs intact. I sewed them on the waistband of another old pair of pants that fit me. I stuffed the legs full of newspaper and attached an old pair of shoes to the end of the legs to look like feet. I put on a crazy top and my sister put all kinds of ponytails in my hair and painted up my face. I looked pretty cool wearing that getup. At least I thought I did.

My mom and sister sure laughed when they saw me. I think I still have the picture mom took of me that night. I went to school for the Halloween party and costume judging. I was so excited. I was sure the extra work I put into the costume would pay off. Want to know who won? Was not me I can tell you that. A boy won. He had a costume too. Well, he called it a costume. He had regular clothes on and over top of that, he wore his mom's housecoat and booties, had a few curlers in his hair and put a little bit of cold cream on his face.

The judges made so much over him, laughing and thinking he was funny. They didn't look twice at me. I thought I did see some of them pointing at me though. Of course, this boy had an upper name. I was so disappointed. I could not believe he won with what he wore.

If he had some great costume, I would have understood. But something that he threw together in less than 5 minutes time? I had spent almost 3 days looking for mine and working on it. No one helped me either. After that, competitions like that didn't mean much to me. I never tried to win anything after that. It showed me that it didn't matter what you did, just what your last name was.

As you might have already guessed, I didn't have a "right" last name. Me, I grew up in the lower click. My folks were divorced since I was two and I had very few memories of my dad or should I say Mom's ex-husband. That's all he was to me as he was never around and never was a dad to me. Mom told me little things and I have few memories of him picking us up for his time with us.

I believe it stopped when I was around four years old. My older sister told Mom he drove funny and smelled funny after we stopped somewhere for a "pop". Mom knew what he was doing and I do remember her asking me if I wanted to go with him anymore. My sister gave me a look like, "say NOOO!", so I said "I don't care if I go or not." He never came around after that and we didn't go with him anymore.

My mom struggled to earn enough money to provide for my sister and me. It wasn't that she didn't provide enough, but I know now looking back, that it was a tough time for her. Of course, she had her hurdles to jump too. You just didn't divorce your husband in the sixties and raise kids alone. It was not done.

As a wife, you were supposed to be home keeping up with a house and kids while your husband worked.

You were supposed to have supper waiting hot and ready for when your husband came home after a hard day at work. He was supposed to be the sole breadwinner and Supreme Being in a household. My mom did the unthinkable. She took control and kicked out her husband and got a divorce. Before you start thinking badly of her, she did this for one reason. She did it to have a better life for her kids.

Anyway, I can tell you more about that part later. I just wanted you to know a little about where I grew up; small-town USA. Now I know that most small towns are like the one I grew up in, but I didn't realize that at the time. It is a small community, big enough where you can still get the new and improved conveniences, yet still farm related so you cannot forget your roots. The town is historical and has had a lot of impact on important events in the past.

It was a place where major crime has not yet touched. A town where you can see traditions that mixes the old with the new. It is a place where pride and old ways still exist. Yep, this just meant one thing to a kid. Life was boring with a capital B. Nothing exciting ever happened. My life consisted of school, home, babysitting, school, home, you get the idea. If things didn't happen where I could see them, then to me, it was so out of reach, it might as well have happened in outer space. Life seemed so far away and I was never going to be a part of it. Remember these are the thoughts of a young girl. Pretty boring I know, but all I had for a role model was what I saw on TV or the occasional movie we got to go too.

Things were looking pretty bleak about having an equally boring adulthood. At least that is the way I used to think. I'm not sure when it happened or when I stopped thinking that way. I think life just grabs you and takes you on your way and before you know it, you've changed even when you knew in your heart you wouldn't. As I look back, I can see things happened for a reason. Everything has a purpose and if you let it, everything will work out for the best. I thought I was in for a pretty boring life; a life that would be boring and dull until that very day; the day that changed my whole life forever.

Chapter 2

I remember it like yesterday. See, I was a musician. Or at least, I sure wanted to be. I played the coronet in band and because of a fluke, I got to learn to play bass guitar. Our school started kids out in band in the fifth grade. My older sister had already joined band and I had gone to all of her concerts. I had sat in the audience watching all the kids play the instruments. My mom had said I could do it too when it was my time, and I wanted to pick just the right instrument.

As I watched each person play, I thought about how hard each instrument would be to play. I watched all the woodwinds and figured it would be too hard to play all those keys. I watched the brass and thought about how heavy each instrument was. I even looked at the percussion and knew I was not coordinated enough to do that.

For me, the brass looked like my best bet. I paid attention to each brass instrument. The tuba and baritone looked too big and heavy. The trombone looked too complicated because I didn't see how they knew where to put the slide. As far as the French horn and the trumpet, I liked the looks of the trumpet better, so that was my choice. I figured there were only three buttons, so how hard could that be? I sure had no clue and I found out just how hard it was to play. I didn't know a thing about the lip work that was involved.

I told my mom I wanted to play the trumpet so that was it. She found a friend who had a used coronet for $25.00. It was in her price range, and I was told it was just as good, so that's what I ended up with. Now this coronet had seen its better days when I got it. The brass was tarnished beyond shining and was missing in places. It had a few small dents in it, but they didn't affect the playing. The valves were in good condition and it was still playable, so I was in business.

I remember many times practicing in my room and how discouraged I would be because of how I sounded. I could not for the life of me get the sound I was supposed to. I had the words "Quality over quantity" embedded in my mind, so I tried and tried. Many times, I wanted to throw the thing out the window and forget it. I never gave up because every time I even hinted about quitting, I was told, sure I could quit if I wanted to be lazy. If I wanted to be good like my older sister, then I would keep at it. So, I pretty much figured I was stuck. I tried hard to please my mom and I knew there was no way I could quit.

After a time and after I started to show improvement, I actually enjoyed playing. I would listen to my sound and try to make it as sweet as I could. I would practice my airflow because that sure made a difference in the sound. And they were right. Once you could control the quality of the sound, you could control the quantity of the sound. I was soft where it was needed and I could be loud where it was needed. It wasn't long before I was playing first place music and was at the top of all the trumpet section.

There were few kids who seemed to take music seriously as it was known as an easy credit. Most of the other kids spent the hour messing around and creating havoc in class. I knew if I was seen as a band geek, it would really give the other kids another reason to pick on me. I would secretly love music, but I just couldn't show it. I was serious about practicing and playing, I just couldn't act like it. It was a fine line I walked, but I felt I had to walk it.

While I was playing, I felt like I was flying. I would listen to my sound and no matter what I was any other time, while I was playing, I was beautiful. I was free and I could fly. It didn't matter if anyone else thought this or felt this way. What mattered was I felt this way. I knew it was my time to shine even if I was the only one who saw or felt it. It might be kind of silly, but it was the way I felt back then. It kept me going. It was my release and at the time, it made everything worthwhile. It was the start of my real love of music. I didn't know it, but it was a good time for me.

I used to play taps for the local American Legion. The high school band teacher got me involved because I was one of her top players. I really enjoyed getting out and playing because it was a chance to shine. I really felt like I was doing something great and the little money I earned doing didn't hurt either.

One Memorial Day, I was asked to go out with the Legion and play taps at every cemetery they did a 21-gun salute in. Mom asked me when we got to the cemetery where her brother was buried, would I think of him when I played? I said I would and I did.

As I got ready to play, I thought about only him, how he gave his life for his country and how much my mom missed him. I started to play only thinking of him and I have to say I think that was the prettiest I ever sounded. Even the other people listening commented on how good I played. It made me feel good to do that for my mom and I was glad to do it for his memory as well.

As worn as my old coronet was, I could sure make it sing. As I said before, I always worked on the quality first. I didn't play anything without really feeling it and I was told it sounded very good. One day I was in the band room just practicing by myself when my teacher came out of her office. She had her brand new Getzen trumpet in her hand. She asked me to play the same music only to use her trumpet. I did and she said it sounded beautiful.

It would have been great to have a better trumpet back then, but it really didn't bother me. I believed my love of music shined through when I played. It didn't matter if the instrument I had was of quality or not. It might have made it easier, but I don't think I would have made it better. Years later, my husband bought me a silver Getzen trumpet. I wish I had that back in high school and he told me if we dated back then, he would have busted his backside to buy me a better trumpet. I guess I missed out back then, but at the time, it didn't matter.

I did grow up with music in my life. My mom loved country music and listened to it every chance she got. She had a pretty good collection of records and if there was nothing good on TV or on the radio, we'd fire up the high-FY and play some of her records. Hee Haw and the Grand Ole Opry were staples in our home and we even listened to the Lawrence Welk show a lot.

Secretly, I loved the guitar and wanted to play so bad. We didn't have any instruments like that, so there was no way I could ever learn. My mom's boyfriend did have an old Martin guitar he let me strum on from time to time, so I did have a way of trying my hand at playing. I found out it was pretty hard to keep my fingers on all those strings and making it have any kind of a good sound. It didn't keep me from trying but it didn't mean I was any good either.

It wasn't until middle school that I got a chance to learn how to play bass guitar. It was at my practice session one day with a band teacher of whom I have great respect for. At the time, I didn't know what was happening. Turned out, there was a gal in my class who was trying to quit band. She was the daughter of the high school principle and definitely was one of the upper clicked kids. The band teacher was trying desperately to talk her into not quitting.

She played percussion and I don't know if she didn't like it, if it was boring for her or if it was just plain too hard. Whatever her reasons were, she was not giving in to the teacher. I heard him say, he needed someone to learn to play bass guitar. I know he was hoping she'd change her mind for him. But without waiting for her answer, I spoke up and said I'd be willing to learn if she didn't want to. All I heard was the word guitar. I loved listening to others play and remember I secretly wanted to learn myself. I had no idea that because the word bass was attached, it was a whole different ball of wax than what I was seeing on TV.

To this day, I still remember the look he gave me. It was like he was saying or even screaming, "Shut up! I want her to learn, not you." I remember her saying, "There, now you got someone to learn, you don't need me." And out she walked. She never came back to the band room after that day. That was the start of my bass guitar playing world.

The band teacher looked at me and said, "Well, I guess if you really want to learn, I will teach you." At first, it was hard. I didn't really understand what it was. After I started to realize the importance of the bass and what it was for, I started to have a little more coordination and confidence in what I was doing, it wasn't too bad.

The teacher was trying to groom students to play in the school's jazz band. He picked students who seemed to stand out and excel above the others. He wanted kids who showed a drive to learn and still have the sound he was looking for. I'm not sure he would have picked me for bass, but since I volunteered and showed a desire to learn, I was it. He worked with me and I started to learn music for the Jazz Band.

Since I already knew how to read treble clef for trumpet, it made learning to read bass clef a lot more difficult. I kept getting the two mixed up. It just seemed so confusing to me. I kept reverting back to treble clef and kept playing everything all wrong.

So, I started to do what any other normal kid would do. I started to "cheat". Now I don't mean the cheating when it comes to looking at another kid's paper and copying the answers. I mean the cheating involved in making something more possible by taking the easier road than the harder one you really should go down. Since I couldn't seem to learn, I had to do something to help myself play.

I started writing a code on all my music. For all you non-musicians, this just involved two numbers. I would write fractions under each note. The first number would indicate which string and the second number would indicate which fret. The bass has only four strings and those little horizontal bars you see on the neck of any guitar are called a fret. So, it would read something like this, 4/3 meaning forth string, third fret and so on.

I think my first band teacher grew tired of trying to teach me to read bass clef music and let me mark up the music because it was easier. I always used pencil and wrote real light, so it was easy to erase it when we were done playing the piece, so it wasn't a problem. I did this with every piece of music we played all the way up to my junior year.

My new band teacher (my 3rd) actually told me she was tired of me marking up the music and was going to make me learn to read bass clef it was the last thing she did. Since I always tried hard to please my teachers, I agreed to try. I even gave up playing my coronet for almost a full year and took up the baritone for two reasons. Number one, it would help me with reading bass clef, number two, we were short kids playing it and the teacher needed the sound for the music we were playing.

Even though I was giving up a first chair spot playing coronet, I figured I would still be playing first chair because we didn't have any other baritone players. It was just an opportunity to learn another instrument. By this time, I had a love for music and wanted to learn any other instrument I could get my hands on. I would have loved to continue this and maybe go to college for music. I wasn't sure if I could, but I figured it wouldn't hurt to have the experience.

Anyway, throughout these years, I was getting better and better with my coordination needed for my bass playing. I knew I couldn't sing to save my soul, so my playing had to come first. As long as I had my music marked, I could play the piece. As I was starting to learn to read bass clef, I felt I was improving by leaps and bounds.

By the time my day came, I was in this frame of mind. I knew I wasn't a great bass player, but my aspirations were great. I had grown up listening to all of the oldies of country music. I loved the sounds of the guitars and really wanted one day to be in a real country music band. Of course, I knew I couldn't play by ear and there was probably no way I could ever remember all the songs one needed to play to be in such a band, but that didn't stop me from dreaming.

It was the day that I believe my whole life was changed. For my love of playing, I always wanted my own guitar. I secretly dreamed of owning a Rickenbacker. I had asked around and everyone said they were the best you could buy. I knew if you wanted quality, something that would last, you had to buy the best. Probably one of the most expensive bass guitars there were. Realistically, I knew I could never afford one. Besides of them being very heavy, it just was not in the cards for me to own one. I remember always looking in the paper in hopes of finding one somewhere cheap enough for me to afford.

One day, I remember, my ship came in. As I looked through the local paper, I saw a huge ad for a scratch and dent sale at a local music store. It said there was a closeout on all kinds of makes and models of brand-new guitars that had some small defect in it making them sell them for much less. The prices advertised were with in my price range. Oh boy was I excited!

After much talk...okay...pleading with my mom, she finally agreed to go with me to see if there was one, I could afford. I told her I would pay for it out of my own money, that it wouldn't cost her a dime. She agreed, but I would have a spending limit. She had it in her mind the money I had worked for and saved was to be used for college only. She hated the idea of me spending any money I had in the bank. It was like taking steps backwards and she couldn't stand that. I guess in her mind, she was just trying to look out for my best interests. I can't blame her for that.

I can't tell you the excitement I felt. At the time, I was a kid who was pretty awkward. I felt I was very much overweight. I seemed to be built heavier than the rest of my friends. I felt like I was ugly and really had a terrible case of acne. No matter what I did, my skin seemed to be always broke out. I was very self-conscious about it. Mom even took me to a dermatologist. I felt like where ever I went, all eyes were on the terrible condition of my skin. My coordination was not great and my body had problems that kept me from doing things that normal kids could do. I felt like I was a walking nightmare.

A few months before this, I got involved with a martial art form called Kempo. A friend of mine told me about the class and asked me to go with when she checked it out. I went and was impressed with what I seen. I liked the movements and really liked the way it was being taught. Again, I pleaded with my mom to let me take lessons and again promised I would pay for them on my own. My older sister took dance lessons and when I brought this up and asked "Why couldn't I do what I was interested in like she did?" I'm not sure if she paid the bill or if my mom paid the bill, but it did help to get her to agree to let me take the class.

Taking this class and learning the art not only helped my self-confidence, but it helped my flexibly as well. Flexible is something which I just never was. I spent a lot of time stretching and practicing the movements. I started to improve and I enjoyed doing it so much. I could even sit with my legs straight out in front of me which is something I could never do before.

I looked forward to the lessons. I put a lot of energy into learning what I needed to know. I even got into sparing and the fighting aspect. Although I never thought I was vicious enough to survive any major fight, I liked to go through the motions. It made me feel good to be able to do it. After I broke my first board, I was flying. I could not believe I had that strength in me. It was a good time in my life and made a huge difference in my confidence.

The Kempo teacher even let me go with him to see an actual tournament in Chicago. I was very excited to get to go because I wanted to see first hand what it was all about. It just had me in awe! When we got there and walked into the auditorium, I didn't know were to look first. There were about at least 6 fighting rings all going at once.

There were classes for men and women for fighting. Someone was demonstrating katas and the use of different weapons I have never even seen before. There was so much noise with people talking, hollering and clapping; it was deafening. My teacher wanted me to pay attention to the women fighters so I could decide if I wanted to participate or not.

As I watched them fight, I could see that a lot of the women fought more viscously than the men did. After watching for a while, I knew it was not for me. There was no way I could ever survive in the ring and fight like that. The experience was very enjoyable though. I believe my favorite part was watching the kata and the weaponry demonstrations. That I figured I could do once I learned them and had lots of practice.

On the way home, I thanked the teacher for taking me with him. I added that the fighting was cool, but just not for me. After I explained it was just too violent for me. I didn't mind sparing in his Do Jo, but that was more intense than I wanted. He laughed and told me as soon as we walked in, he knew it wasn't going to work with me fighting. I laughed to and told him I wouldn't mind doing the katas or the weapons, I just wasn't good enough to compete.

Anyway, to get to the point, the day of the sale was on a day that I was supposed to go to a Kempo lesson. When I told my instructor, I wouldn't be to Saturday's lesson, he wanted to know why. I told him because I was going to go buy a bass guitar. I was so proud because I was paying for it on my own. He seemed surprised. He told me he had a job in a real band if I could play bass. As excited as I already was, I skyrocketed. Right away, I told him I could not play by ear, that I needed sheet music to be able to play. He said not to worry, that they would try me out anyway.

I also remember my fear was just about as great as my excitement. I just could not get over the fact that not only was I going to achieve my goal of actually owning my very own bass guitar, but now I was going to have a chance to play in a real band. It was so unbelievable; I could hardly contain myself. Things like this only happened to folks who were in stories in books or on TV. Could it be, was it true that I was in a story with a happy ending?

Chapter 3

It was an October morning; October 2 to be exact. The day was bright and clear. I remember being so excited during the twenty-five-minute drive to the music store. All I could think about was...a bass guitar...MY bass guitar. I even had an idea of what I wanted.

To please my mom, I had asked everyone I knew who played music about the good quality guitars. She didn't want me to buy a piece of junk. She also knew it wasn't good to buy something that wasn't made right. When I talked with my band teacher, I pretty much had the name of Fender in my head. It was the brand of guitar all the schools had. I'm not sure he believed I was actually buying one because he didn't seem to want to talk to me about it.

I think maybe he was still mad at me for taking that girl's place playing bass. I never had any proof, because he always treated me good. He never talked down to me and the only time he chewed on us was when we deserved it because someone was messing around when they shouldn't have. Nothing was ever directed at me personally, so I really can't complain about the way I was treated.

I always liked him and had a great respect for him

and tried to please him. I was really sad when he later passed away from cancer. He taught so many kids to play and was an icon for us all. Years later, when he died, he was greatly missed. I still think about him from time to time and remember him fondly.

From the second I walked through the music store's door; I saw the bass guitar that I wanted. It was beautiful. Of course, I couldn't see what name brand it was, but it sure caught my eye. It was sunburst blue, my favorite color, which turned to black in the back and it had a white pick guard. I pointed to it and told my mom, that's the one I wanted.

She kind of laughed because how could I tell from such a distance. I knew she thought I was silly for saying I wanted that one without seeing it close up. As I walked over to it so I could see it closer; I stood for a few minutes just gazing at it. I asked the clerk if I could see that one pointing up at it. As he handed it to me, it just felt so good to hold it. Just the feel of it felt great. I could tell instantly it was lighter than the school's Fender. I remember thinking, this is a good thing.

They let me go in a practice room to see if I'd like the sound. After plugging it in and playing a few notes, I knew I was right. As I listened, it just reinforced what I knew instantly. It was a Washburn. It was way different than a Fender in make and weight. Mom asked me how I liked it and what brand was it. She was concerned it wasn't as good of quality as a Fender. She made me call my band teacher to see if that was a quality name too. He reassured her, telling her that was a good quality guitar too so she agreed I could buy it.

The bass actually was lighter and my favorite color, I was amazed because I even thought the sound quality was better. The only "defect" it had was a small dent and break in the paint job on the back of the body. Other than that, the guitar was perfect. I didn't care about the so-called defect because I knew that in time, I'd probably put more "defects" in it through use, so I told Mom, that was not a problem for me.

She kept asking me if I wanted to look at another guitar. I guess she thought I should try to play some of the other guitars they had to be sure it was the right one. I told her nope, this is the one. I knew I didn't need to waste my time playing those other guitars. She finally agreed and after some more purchases of a case to protect it, a cleaning spray, a cloth, white strap and an extra set of strings, I brought my new baby home.

The pride I felt was sure amazing. I spent so many hours practicing it, polishing it and just plain looking at it. It was overwhelming to realize it was all mine. Because I even bought it with my own money, made my buttons burst. I had never owned anything so expensive or so beautiful before in all my life. It was the most important purchase I ever made for myself.

I had bought things on my own before but nothing that was this expensive. I remember saving my pennies, nickels and dimes so I could buy a present for my mom. I remember my sister and I were proud as punch when we saved our money to buy her a pitcher and glass set for Mother's Day. It was a green glass pitcher with six matching glasses. I think we only paid 2 or 3 dollars for it, but for us it was a fortune. I remember wrapping it and being so proud.

It was such a good feeling watching her open it. She made so much out of getting it that even made us feel better. Through the years I think the glasses got broken one by one. When she passed, she had a few glasses left along with the pitcher. I kept the pitcher and still have it today. The memory attached to it brings a smile every time I think of it.

I bought other things for mom through the years, but nothing felt as good as being able to buy that first present for mom with my own money. We didn't make much in those days, just a few cents each week that was our allowance. My sister got more than I did because she was older. I figured it was because she did more chores because her list was always longer than mine. It didn't bother me none because it was just the way it was. Mom never left for work without leaving us a note with each of our names on it and a list of chores under each name.

We knew if we didn't have those chores done by the time she got home, there would be heck to pay. It was just easier to be sure the jobs were done than to take the blunt of her anger for not having it done. We would scurry around the house making sure they were done and all things were put in their place before she walked through the door. Sometimes if something was not done that was not on the list, she'd get angry because she felt we should have seen that it needed to be done and just gone ahead and done it anyway.

It was an automatic thing to go through the house to be sure everything was in its place at least 10 minutes before we knew she would be home. Neither one of us wanted what would come if we didn't. We had full respect or maybe I should say fear of our mother.

If she became angry for whatever reason, the punishment would go like this. At the realization you did something wrong, she would yell at you. Very loudly and it usually made you feel about 2 inches tall. You felt horrible for doing whatever it was you did. This usually went on for about a week. Nothing you could do would be right. The next week you would get the silent treatment. She wouldn't talk to you unless it was to tell you to do something or to tell you what you were doing wrong.

The third week, you would get grounded for something else you did. She would say that since you were already bad and she couldn't take the unruliness, would say the proper punishment would be to get grounded. You were not allowed to go anywhere but home or to school. It just was not worth the punishment, so we usually did our best to avoid it. Although sometimes it seemed I just couldn't avoid it no matter what I did.

Of course, with me being the youngest, mom always took my sister's word on what happened or what was done and by whom. I have my own opinions on why this was true but there was never any concrete proof. She never verbally admitted anything, but her actions spoke loud and clear to me.

I had no chance to ever tell my side if there was a side. If I had done something wrong or my sister thought I had done something wrong, I didn't have any chance of telling my side and being seen as telling the truth. She would never believe me and most times wouldn't take the time to even listen. She took what my sister said to be the God's honest truth.

I remember playing with a small bouncy ball. The little rubber ball you got for a nickel out of one of those gum machines. You didn't have to throw it very hard for the little thing to bounce all over the place. I was playing with it by myself, bouncing it all over the house when it bounced up and hit the dining room light. It had a cover on it that had this crack in it. I know it had a crack in it because I would often look up and see it and wonder how it got that way.

After the ball hit it, my sister told me to be careful or else I'd break something. She looked at the light and said, "See, you broke the light cover." I told her I did not break it that it was already broken before the ball hit it. She argued with me and said she was going to tell mom I broke it. I really didn't worry about it because I knew it was broken before. I thought for sure mom would not be angry.

Like usual, I was wrong. Mom took my sister's side and I got spanked and grounded for breaking the light cover. I tried to tell her it was broken already but she wouldn't listen because she was so sure that even if it was, I still broke it in the first place. I was getting the idea then that my sister's only purpose in life was to get me in trouble with my mom.

Something happened after that which proved what I was beginning to see. As I told you, I secretly wanted to learn to play guitar. Since I didn't have a real guitar, I tried to make a pretend guitar. I had this red painted stick that was actually a doll rod that went to something I had no clue of what it was. It was just a wooden stick that I played with. I used it for several purposes. When I played with my marbles, I would get tired of playing like I should, I would pretend I was playing pool and it was my pool cue. When I got tired of that, it was a play gun and I played army. When I got tired of that and if I could get my hands on any type of rubber band, it was a guitar.

One day I found this huge rubber band that was long and thick. I was so happy. I had finally found a rubber band that would stretch the whole length of the stick. I wouldn't have to try to hold it with one hand and strum with the other. So, I tried stretching the band to go on the stick from end to end. The thing kept snapping off, but I knew if I tried hard enough, it would work. I was busy working on it and not really paying any attention to where my sister was in the room.

Many times, I would lose myself in my own imagination and didn't have any clue as to what was going on around me. I was in my own little world busy imagining how much fun it would to be playing my "new" guitar. I worked so hard to try to stretch this rubber band over both ends of this red stick. I almost had it when it snapped and flew off the end of the stick. As I tried to see where it landed so I could go get it and keep trying, it ended up by hitting my sister in the back.

She turned around and hollered at me and said, "You did that on purpose!" Of course, I didn't, but no amount of talking would clear my name. My mom wouldn't even listen to me. She just grabbed me, spanked me and told me to go to my room. I was grounded on the spot for trying to "hurt" my sister. Of course, the punishment didn't end there.

We had planned to go to the movies that night and since I was so "bad", I wasn't allowed to go. I had to stay home alone while they went and got to see the movie. Since we didn't have a lot of money, it was a huge treat to get to go anywhere like that. It really hurt when I was not allowed to go too. To make matters worse, my sister did nothing but brag about how good the movie was and flaunted her candy she got while at the movies in front of me. Because I was bad, I was not allowed to even have any of the candy from the movie house.

I was heartbroken. I felt so abandoned and unloved. I knew after that it didn't matter what I did or how I did it. I would always be "bad" and I would never be believed no matter if I told the truth or not. I didn't start lying or anything like that because I still had an overwhelming urge or need to please my mother. It made me try harder and harder to please her. Not that I ever succeeded, but it didn't stop me from trying.

I usually got punished no matter what, so I just took it as that is what life was and dealt with it. I didn't think it was right, but didn't spend too much time on it until I was alone at night in bed when I could think about what happened during the day. It all was a part of forming how I thought about myself and how I acted. I guess it just groomed me to try as hard as I could to please mom and those who were in charge of me to keep my backside out of trouble. Not sure it always worked, but I sure did try. Still deep down I was beginning to think I was bad and no one would see different meaning I would never be better.

Anyway, back to my story. After I made my big purchase of my bass, I insisted on playing it instead of the school's Fender in all the concerts and practices. Sometimes I thought it was a mistake, because it sure was heavy to carry back and forth from home to the school. We lived almost four blocks or so from the school. It wasn't a long distance, but it seemed longer when you had something heavy to carry.

That was one of the reasons why I picked the coronet as the instrument I wanted to play. Because it was light and I knew I wouldn't have much trouble carrying it back and forth. Sometimes my friends would help me and take turns carrying it to school. Turns out I didn't have long to carry it by myself anyway. I even made my boyfriend bring it to school in his truck so I could have my picture taken with it in my senior yearbook photos.

Boyfriend? Did I say boyfriend? Oh yes... I guess I am back to the day that changed my life forever. See, in buying that fateful beautiful new bass guitar, it gave way to that day when I met him; the one true love of my life. The only partner I would ever want to live my life with. This man would be the father of my children. Yes, the day and actions that changed my whole life. I just had no idea of how much it really would change.

Chapter 4

I told you a little of what I was when I grew up; small town gal, small town life. My life is really no worse than anyone else and definitely not any better. I don't want to say that any life is a mistake but sometimes I wonder about my own. In my frame of mind then, I do think I considered myself as to being a mistake. I could never seem to please anyone nor could I seem to do anything right. Now of course, I know different, but then I was not so sure. I guess I didn't have my adult mind as I like to call it.

I was born to a young unwed mother. From what I was told, she had no way of raising or keeping a baby, so she gave me up for adoption. I guess from there I went to stay at a foster home for about 3 months until my mom adopted me. Mom had suffered a tubal pregnancy and could not have kids of her own when she was younger.

She told me she went to the doctor because she wasn't feeling good. The doctor was sure the trouble was appendicitis. She kept telling him, "I am positive it is NOT appendicitis." He wouldn't listen and scheduled her for surgery. It was during this surgery when they found she was pregnant. A baby had started to grow in one of her tubes. She told me the doctor had nothing to say to her when they told her what was wrong.

She told them again, "See, I told you it wasn't appendicitis!" She showed me the scar and let me tell you medicine has come a long way. It was one heck of a scar! It went the total length down her belly and was still so red and angry looking even after all those years. Yes, medicine sure has improved.

Mom was married to a man for almost 23 years. I'm not sure if it started out as a good marriage or not. Mom never really talked much about it. All I do know is her marriage went bad. I remember her telling me about the fights she would get into with him. She said during the day, she was home alone and would cook a lot of food for supper. She would keep it hot as long as she could and then she would get angry because he wasn't home.

In her anger, she would throw the food away because it was all dried out and ruined from being in the oven so long. Then she would give up waiting for him and go to bed. He'd come home sometime late and wake her up. He'd be drunk and want something to eat. He would holler, "Where is my supper?" She'd get up and yell right back, "It's in the garbage, you can eat it from there!" He would respond with, "Make me something new!" She would refuse and the fight was on. It ended with him beating her up and sometimes choking her out. She would say to me that she threw a lot of food away, so I think that was the same as her admitting she got beat up a lot.

I know she had a lot of plans for her life. She said they had bought this farm outside of the city with the idea of having a home for foster kids. Since she couldn't have her own kids, it was her way of getting what she wanted. I'm not sure why they never did that only I know they didn't live on that farm for long. She told me they bought a lot of places, fixed them up and then had to sell them. I never thought about asking her more about it. I guess it will be information I will never find out the answer to.

Mom always told me she wanted kids and since she couldn't have them, she always wanted to adopt. She would talk and talk about it. Her husband only agreed to let her adopt because he knew it would be something for her do to that would occupy her time. I don't think he had any intention on sticking around and being a real father.

Her first adoption worked out for the best. She had a niece who was a mite on the wild side. The story on this one was kind of strange the way it happened. This niece was seeing a married man then the news of her expecting a baby came along. As a for being with a married man, her punishment was she was not allowed to keep her baby. Her father, my mom's brother, was going to make her give up the baby. He didn't know what else to do with her. After hearing about the predicament, mom offered to adopt the baby so at least a family member would be raising the baby. My uncle agreed and it was done.

Very few questions were asked and few requirements had to be made. I guess after the niece gave up my sister, the guy she was seeing left his wife and they were married. They had two more girls and a boy. So, in reality, my sister has three full blooded siblings that she really never knew personally. She knew of their existence, who they were and where they were, but I don't think she ever really cared.

They didn't have much contact with her as she grew up and from what I understand; she really has no need or drive to know them. I think this is sad when you think about it. But I've come to look at it like this; to each their own. If they don't want to take any time worrying about it, then I shouldn't waste my time either.

About the time my sister turned about 4 years of age, my mom wanted to adopt another child. She felt it would be better if there were at least two of us. She really wanted a big family and she knew by now this was the only way she would ever come close to that reality was by adopting more children. I was told that at the foster home, when they came to pick me up, she asked my sister if they should bring me home. My sister said, "Yes, let's take her home." So, they did.

I guess the adoption requirements back then were pretty lax. Mom has told me the only question they asked her when they adopted my sister was, "Will she have her own bedroom?" When she adopted me, the only question was, "How will the older child react to the baby?" Had they really looked into the situation, I'm not sure any adoption would have been approved.

Not that my mother was a bad person mind you. Actually, she was a great person; hard working and honest as the day was long. It was her husband who wouldn't have made the grade. He was an alcoholic; a very bad one in fact. I'm told he came from a long line of alcoholics. I don't know much about that side of the family because after the divorce, his side disowned my mother. They wouldn't have a thing to do with us or even acknowledge we were alive.

From the stories I am told, the situation before the divorce was not a good one. Her husband had several milk truck businesses that he just plain drank away. Instead of coming home with his paycheck, he'd go straight to the bar and drink away the majority of it. Remember the many nights, she kept supper warm for him and ended up throwing it away because she was angry, he was not home?

Some nights he just plain didn't come home. She told me, that sometimes she thought those nights were better when he didn't come home than the ones when he did. He was usually always drunk and they would fight and he would start to beat her. It just reinforced my belief of the only reason he even agreed to any adoptions was because he thought it would keep my mom busy and tied down at home if she had a couple of kids to raise.

This is what led me to believe he didn't have any intentions on raising us himself let alone being there for us. My mom just got to the point where she knew that things would not get better. In fact, things would just get worse. Several times she tried helping him to overcome his sickness. She sent him away to get cooked out. Each time he'd come back ornery and mean as ever. He would say no one was going to keep him from drinking again. I guess he just plain wanted it that bad.

I don't have many memories of those early years. I only know what I was told. I heard tell we lived on many different farms and houses. On one of these farms, Mom said we had this cow. She was a Hereford cow. I'm not sure what they did with her or why they had her, but apparently, I was in love with this cow. I would spend many hours hand feeding her and petting her. Her name was Mary Ellen.

To this day whenever I see a Hereford in a field, I will say, "Ohhh, look darling, it's Mary Ellen!" The Big Guy has promised whenever we are able to have our own farm that is the cows we will have. He did impose a strict rule though. I'm not allowed to name or pet our cows at all. If we have any cattle, I was told they will be there for food and not to be the world's oldest tame cattle. I don't know what he is talking about, so we will see what happens.

Anyway, I have always loved animals. Horses were my absolute favorite and I wanted my own in the worst way. I wanted to learn to ride even more. Since Grandma's house had a barn, I could never understand why mom would not let me have a horse. I remember telling her I could keep it in the barn and I'd take care of it. She would just laugh and say no every time I asked.

The only animal I was allowed to have growing up was a cat. Our first cat was a wild thing. One of mom's friends had a lot of cats and she brought us in a kitten. It was pretty wild, but as young as it was it soon got used to us. Mom made us put it out every night, but it could be in the house during the day. I played with the cat for hours. I don't know if I got too rough or if the cat got too rough, but I would usually end up by getting scratched somewhere and then I would be grounded for getting too rough with the cat.

I remember when that cat got sick. The Vet said he had distemper and there was nothing he could do for it. He pretty much figured it would die and didn't have the heart to put the poor thing asleep in front of me. He gave us some medicine and told us to take it home, make sure it got plenty of water to drink and recommended I try to feed it a mixture of peanut butter and honey to try to keep its strength up.

He didn't expect it to last long anyway, but he didn't say that to me. So, we took the poor thing home and mom let it stay on our back porch. I moved my pillow and blankets out there and even slept with the cat getting up every so often to force feed water and the mixture to the sick cat. I must have done something right, because after a time, the cat actually recovered.

He just wasn't the same, because he had lost a lot of weight, he never regained its old strength. He might not have been as strong as he was, but he was alive. Mom still wouldn't let him spend the nights inside, so he continued to get into cat fights. I would keep a bucket of water handy by the door for whenever I heard them fighting. I would run out of the house and try to throw water on the other cat, saving mine. Many times, I succeeded, but sometimes I was too late and he would be torn up.

He ended up by getting sick again and dying. I tried hard again to save him, but it just didn't work. It was a sad day for us all. It rained and even the neighbor's hounds who barked all the time were silent. I remember mom's boyfriend coming over and trying to dig a grave in the yard for him. He asked me where I wanted it. I told him along the side of the yard where he liked to lie, under the lilacs. He tried to dig it by hand, but couldn't get very far because of all the roots from the trees.

He kept looking at me as I watched him trying to dig that hole. He just laid down the shovel and left. He returned a while later with the city backhoe and dug a hole with that. I'm not sure if he got into trouble for using it, but he was the boss. I guess no one made any complaints.

He dug the hole and we had our little service for the cat and we buried him. I always loved that man for that. He could have told a little girl "We are burying that cat in a place that is easier to dig.", but he didn't. He just went ahead and got the job done.

Another memory I had was remembering the lights late one night when I was really young. I don't remember at the time knowing what it meant; I just remember the red lights going round and round. In later years, I was told what it was about. When mom's ex-husband was driving his pickup truck home, he had a slight disagreement with a moving train. He drove his truck right into the side of it. From what mom tells me, he was banged up pretty good. He even had to have a metal plate put in his skull. The doctors told him then, that he would kill himself if he didn't quit his drinking that his organs were not in the best of shape because of the alcohol.

Mom told me she was so afraid when she went to the hospital to see him. He looked like a mummy because he was wrapped in bandages from head to toe. As bad as he was, she didn't even know how he even survived the crash. By all rights, he should have died that night.

Mom even said when he went to court over the charges he received, the lawyer tried to get him to change his ways. I guess mom took us kids to court too and when the lawyer looked at us sitting there in our dresses, he just pointed to us. He told him to look too. He said; "Look at those beautiful little girls sitting there. Can't you see how much they need you?" The lawyer thought the sight of us would be enough to make him change his ways because we really needed him to. Nope. Us sitting there looking all innocent and sweet did not do a darn thing to deter him. As soon as he got out, he went right back to drinking.

Mom had finally had enough. She decided a life without a drunk father who might beat us up anytime he came home was way better than having that kind of father in our lives. She didn't want us to grow up dealing with what an alcoholic brought. She thought long and hard about what she needed to do. You need to remember the time and all her friends and most of the family told her she was crazy and she should just put up with it.

She was so confused she even went to talk to her priest. She told him of what she was dealing with. She told him of her two daughters and what she feared. She asked him what should she do. She later confessed that if he said that she was to honor her marital vows and stay there and put up with it, then that is what she would do. But the priest didn't say that. He told her to pack her bags and get those two girls out of that situation no matter how she had to do to do it. And she was to do it as quick as she could.

So, she listened, left and filed for divorce. Since most of the people around her didn't agree with what she was doing, she moved back to this small town to be closer to the only family she could count on. His side, like I said before, disowned her and would not speak to her or even acknowledge her presence. She had done the thinkable. She divorced one of them. He had three brothers and a sister. Every one of them was instructed not to have a thing to do with mom or us kids.

So, at the time, she did the only thing she knew to do. She struggled and worked as hard as she could to provide for her children. She worked as a waitress and made little money. The thing that rankles me is she knew she needed help and tried to go to Social Services to ask for financial assistance. They told her she made too much money to receive any help from them. How do you earn what a waitress does, be responsible for raising two children and make too much money by yourself? It's beyond me.

She moved back home to be close to her mother and father. My grandma was a sure special person in her own right. This is a lady well worth telling about. My grandma grew up poor as well. I do mean dirt poor. Her own mother died when she was about 14, so she had to grow up fast. I don't know too many details of her life, but I just know it was not an easy one. I do, however, remember the stories my mom told me of her life growing up.

Mom told stories of her having move from one big old rundown farmhouse to another. They had to live in big ole houses so hard to heat in the winter that they would have to shut off rooms they didn't really need to keep warm. Ever hear of the saying, "Pig in the Parlor?" Well, when my mom was little, she remembers my grandma butchering a hog in the beginning of winter and taking a white sheet and spreading it out on their parlor floor and laying the pig on it.

Since this was one of the closed off rooms, it would stay cold in there so the pig would not spoil. It was like having a huge indoor freezer. The houses back then did not have the insulation or weather stripping to protect the inside from the extreme cold we face in this part of the country. Whenever grandma wanted ham or bacon, she would just simply go in the parlor and cut off whatever she wanted.

Mom told me other stories of how they never had much to eat. She remembered more than once Grandma sent them to school with nothing but popcorn in their lunch pails. This was the only food she could send with them because that was all they had. My mom laughed as she remembered being envied by the other kids. They'd say, "We wish our mom gave us popcorn to eat." The kids wouldn't realize the popcorn was there because it was all they had.

Mom remembers having to do such chores as chopping wood. It would be her job to go out and make kindling for the fire. This was a job she hated because her older sister never had to do it. She remembers a few times of speaking back to her mother and what she got. Her story of one time in particular that stuck with me, stood out in her memory well. She remembered she was mad cause she had to split the wood.

She was outside chopping so wildly; her mother saw her, came out and told her she was doing it wrong. Grandma told her, "What do you want to do?

Cut off your foot?" My mother replied with, "Well if you don't like it, you can do it yourself." Let me tell you, she never said that again. She got it good for that one. You just didn't back talk my grandma. Wasn't proper and she didn't put up with it. You can believe a switch got cut and my mother paid for her sharp tongue.

Another time I was told about was my mom was allowed to go to the next farm to play with a girlfriend. She was told that she could go, but she had to be home before supper. Her friend invited her to stay for supper and since the food was better than what she knew she would get at home, my mom decided to stay. Had she gone home right after supper, she probably still would have been okay, but after supper she still stayed and played till well after dark. She ended up by getting it good that time too. You just plain didn't cross Grandma. What she said was it. Grandma wasn't mean, she just grew up in a time that was hard and it made for hard people. I don't think she knew how to show real tender emotions. She was a no-nonsense type person.

I don't remember too much about my grandpa. The only thing mom would say was he was gone a lot. I'm not sure why, most likely working very low paying jobs. I'm not sure if they got along, but mom was the youngest of four living children. I sit and try to remember details of what she told me and I realize it is hard to recall just what she has told me during the years.

One thing I do remember is hearing how much she hated and grew tired of never having any new clothes or shoes. She said all her shoes were hand-me-downs from her older sister. Mom always blamed the poor condition of her feet when she was older on having to wear shoes that never really fit when she was young. They were already broke in on someone else's feet. The shoes were always well worn by the time she grew into them and were usually very uncomfortable.

Because they didn't have a lot of money, Grandma used to work any job she could for extra cash. She took in laundry and even cooked at a local restaurant. Grandma was also quite resourceful. She would make her own furniture when she needed to. She even made her own kitchen cupboards. One is still in existence in my mom's basement today. I look at it whenever I go down there and marvel at my grandma's abilities.

My mom remembers one Christmas like it was yesterday. She said that Grandma had no money for Christmas presents, so she took a trip to the nearby junk yard. She came home with an old toy wagon someone threw away and fixed it and painted it on Christmas Eve. When my mom awoke and found the "new" wagon, she just could not understand why Santa would bring a wagon when the paint was still wet. She thought he was awful busy and he was probably a mite late with the presents that year.

Yep, my grandma was quite the lady. In my years of being with her and I even asked my mom on this one, I never remember ever hearing her swear. I don't just mean the big swear words, but the little ones such as "heck' and "damn". I think that is something. Whatever happened, whatever she had to deal with, she just did. Without getting upset or angry, it was just life. How many of us can really say that about ourselves now a-days? Even myself, I know that my biggest downfall is talking like a truck driver. I know I do it, and I know I should stop, and I know I want to stop, but do I? Nope…I don't.

I remember a few other things about my grandma. She could make homemade bread. My mom was always complaining she could never make bread anywhere near what Grandma could do. Just the smell of it baking was one of the best smells there was. Awesome! She always had molasses cookies too. It was a treat to go to see Grandma because she always gave you a glass of milk and shared her molasses cookies she kept around. I'm not sure if she bought them or if she made them herself, but they sure tasted good. The quickest way for me to remember Grandma is to eat a molasses cookie.

My grandma was always pretty active about what was happening in our town. She listened to the radio every day and would write letters about anything she felt was worthwhile. She was even instrumental in getting the city to make the old fire department building into a senior citizen center. She never got any recognition for that one, but I know what she did because she talked about it all the time.

Grandma loved to make things. She had artificial flowers that she made into arrangements. She used to make her own Christmas decorations with fake pearls and ribbons and such with Styrofoam balls. These ornaments would get sold at local fairs and such for extra money. They turned out really pretty and I remember always having them on the Christmas tree.

She also loved to crochet. She would sit and make

pillows and Afghans like you wouldn't believe. Even after she got older and started losing her eyesight, she would still sit and crochet. It didn't matter if she could see or not because her quality never changed. She would sit there and talk to you, and have her ball of yarn in a bowl so she didn't lose it. Her hands would be busy making something beautiful. She never looked at what she was doing because she couldn't see it; she just looked at you and talked away. It always seemed to turn out and she felt looking at you was more important anyway. She would sit for hours and do this.

There would also be a radio playing in the background. She would stop and pay close attention to the obituary reports. I always thought this was pretty morbid and never understood why she did it. I asked her why she listened once and she said "So I can hear if I know anyone who passed so I can say goodbye to them proper." As a kid, you don't think of these things, but as I'm older, I do the same as she did. I always stop what I'm doing to listen when I hear this same report to see if I know anyone who passed so I can say goodbye proper too.

It wasn't that she didn't have her own heart aches. I know she lost at least two children as infants. As poor as she was, she could not afford to buy a plot to bury her children. They were buried at the foot of someone else because they were so small. Mom always wondered where they were buried. Because they didn't keep that accurate of records, it was dang near impossible to find out. Mom inquired at the cemetery several times to see if they knew where the infants were buried. They could never seem to tell her because they just plain didn't know themselves. All we know is they were buried somewhere in that cemetery.

Grandma was also a Gold Star Mother. This is pretty prestigious as there was not many left in town. Her son gave his life in WWII on Omaha Beach, Normandy, France. He was shot in the groin area by a sniper. His brother-in-law was there and seen it happen. They had to knock him out to keep him from running out to save Grandma's son.

Of course, even if he did, he couldn't have saved him, because of where he was hit. He was bound to die even if he got medical attention. That did not make it any easier to handle. My uncle was a POW and died in a German hospital. He was buried in a German Hospital Cemetery amongst many German soldiers. After a little while, he moved to the cemetery that overlooks Omaha Beach. About 5 years later, Grandma received a letter asking her if she wanted his remains to be returned to her.

An armed guard accompanied a casket that was brought back and reburied in the church cemetery. Mom told me she never knew if his remains were really in that casket or not. The guard never left the casket until it was laid to rest in the ground. She told me she often wished she could have looked inside to see. I told her it was probably best she didn't because it would be so decomposed it might give her nightmares.

I also thought it would be better for her to remember him as he was anyway. His name is listed on the Memorial at the city park and is announced at every Memorial Day Celebration. I know it was a terrible blow to Grandma in losing her son. It has to be the worst thing ever to deal with. That is one thing in this world that is not right. Children should bury parents; parents should never bury children.

Grandma spent her life trying to survive and paying for numerous small life insurance plans. These plans always seem to nickel and dime her for as long as I could remember. Funny thing was, when she died, not a one of those policies paid any money. Turns out, she had out lived each and every one of them. It's kind of sad when you stop to think of it. All that money she scrimped and saved to pay the premium on all those policies, she could have bought something nice. Something that would have made her life easier or something that would have made her happy.

Grandma helped my mom a lot. She watched us kids while mom worked. We lived in a few houses that mom rented before coming to live with Grandma, but it just never seemed to work for her. Mom never seemed happy. Grandma lived in her house all alone. It wasn't a huge house, but it was home. After a while, my grandma decided she would buy a trailer and put it on the other side of the lot she owned and live there while mom and us kids lived in her house.

It was just a small 2-bedroom one story house. When Grandma bought it, it had no windows and had a tree through the roof. I even have pictures of what it looked like. There was the house, a small shed, an outhouse and a barn on 3 town lots. Grandma fixed it up as best as she could. As I told you before, she even built her kitchen cupboards. She replaced the windows and fixed the roof. The cupboards Grandma built stayed in the house until Mom remodeled and bought new ones.

I remember when Grandma moved. She had a huge sale because all her furniture wouldn't fit in the trailer. I remember having her belongings she wanted to sell out on the lawn and all these people were there buying it. The money helped her pay for the trailer, I guess. I didn't like all these people rifling through things like that; didn't seem right to me. Grandma kept a few things she really wanted, but most of her antiques went. I'm not sure she got what it was worth, but I guess she was satisfied.

I remember when Grandma started getting sick. It seemed like Mom was constantly taking her to the doctor. She would tell them what her symptoms were and her doctor just could not find anything wrong. I remember hearing the doctors telling my mom, Grandma's sickness was all in her head. Even so, she had a TV tray full of medications that she had to take every day. I wondered why he gave them to her if there was nothing wrong with her.

As I looked at them, I was amazed at the number of bottles and ask, "How do you remember what you have to take?" She did explain what each and every one was for and how many she took. I was just in awe how she kept everything straight.

Over the next few years, she went from home to the hospital, to a nursing home to home to a hospital, to a caregiver's house, to a hospital, to a nursing home and back home again. I remember mom taking her to the doctor just to be told again that everything she felt was all in her head and nothing was wrong. Yet she would sit up all night coughing and not being able to sleep.

For all those times Grandma was in a nursing home, I hated it. I hated everything about it; how it looked, the smell, the sounds, everything. It just seemed like a place old people went to die alone. Grandma would tell me how she didn't like it either. She'd tell me how mean her roommates would be to her. She couldn't help coughing and her roommate would get so angry she'd yell at her and wake her for meanness whenever Grandma did fall asleep.

It was a horrible place and I hated going. I hated it so very much; I told mom one day, "I promise NEVER to put you in a place like that." I meant it. Mom laughed and said, "Yea, we will see what happens." That's one thing about me. I never make a promise I don't keep.

I remember Mom taking Grandma to the hospital that last time. She was gone for most of the night and it was pretty late when Mom came back home alone. I remember her telling us kids that grandma died. It wasn't that I didn't love my grandma; I just didn't know how I was to feel. I remember the whole family coming and going to the wake and funeral. My aunt came and even stayed for a few days. I remember having to share a bed with her and she laid there beside me crying and telling me how much she missed Grandma.

Funny thing was, I just couldn't remember my aunt around all that much to actually be missing her like that. I remember mom crying. When mom's boyfriend came in and asked how Grandma was, I remember his reaction to the answer of "She died." I'm not sure Grandma even liked him, but I know he respected her. I think he left the house so us kids wouldn't see him cry. I think I cried, but not a lot. I just didn't understand. I didn't know what it was that I felt. Then, life went on.

Mom was left 1/3rd of Grandma's house and all her things. Mom was faced with the choice of what to do. Should she sell and move or should she buy the other 2/3's of the house from her brother and her sister. The decision was made. She talked with her brother and her sister and they were all too happy to agree. Mom bought the place lock stock and barrel.

Later on, I would know that Mom had a few hurt feelings on this. She felt a little betrayed because all those years, her brother and her sister were nowhere around when grandma needed help and care. Mom was there. She did it all. I know what she felt. I do think she deserved the house for her years of care and effort because she always did what she could to help Grandma when she was sick. I guess it don't matter now because it is all said and done. But how you think things should be is not always how they are.

Years later, I remember mom and my aunt having a big blow out. My aunt and her daughter came to visit for a spell. Even though they were there, Mom still had to go work to pay bills. When she was gone to work during the day, they would go through things that was stored in the attic, shed and barn. The things they found that they wanted, they packed up and loaded in their car. Now, I know if they had asked, I'm sure mom would have gladly given it to them. It was the fact that they went and took stuff without her permission or her knowledge is what fried my mom.

I remember her coming home and seeing some boxes and other things in the back of their car. When she looked and realized what it was, she blew; big time. She told them, point blank, that she when bought the place and they wanted to get rid of it quick, and didn't care about anything then. She bought everything that was there and they had no more rights to it. She asked them where were they when Grandma needed care? Where were they when bills were needed to be paid or repairs that needed to be done?

Now, they come back after all these years and think they have rights to grandma's belongings without asking her first? She told them to hit the road and not to come back! She was so mad I believed she could have spit nails. I cannot really blame her for being so angry. I think I would be the same way. I do remember they never spoke to each other for a few years after that. Eventually things calmed down and they started speaking again.

We were, however, not much of what I would call close family. My family was my grandma, my mom and my sister. Everyone else was just acquaintances; folks we just visited every so often. Oh yea, of course there was my mom's boyfriend. Story had it that they dated before she married her husband. When he went off to the service and was overseas, she Dear-Johned him and married her husband. I never found out until just a bit ago why she did this. I never had the nerve to ask, figured it was none of my business.

One day while we were talking about things, she finally told me. Turns out that they were engaged before he left and while he was overseas, word got back to mom that he was dating two different gals. One was an English lady and the other was an Irish lady. One he was even planning on bringing back home when he got out of the service. Mom told me that he had hurt her and it made her angry. She felt like why should she wait for him and be true to him when he wasn't true to her. So, she sent the Dear-John letter breaking up with him and married her husband.

Now in case you are wondering, I do not refer to her husband as my father. I might have hinted at this before, but I think I best say it clear. Yes, his name is listed on my birth certificate as my father, but I can tell you, he definitely was not my father. I don't feel that way just because of the fact he was not my blood father. I believe it takes more than blood to be a father or a mother for that matter. Any sap can conceive and give birth to a child.

It takes a real mother and a father to be there for the child through thick and thin. Blood has nothing to do with it. If you're a true mother or father to a child, it means you give them unconditional love. You are there for them 24/7. It doesn't mean you are perfect and know how to handle problems that come with raising a child. All that matters is you are there and try the best you can do simply because you love your child.

Just because my mother's ex-husband has his name on my birth certificate does not mean he is my dad. That is where it stops. He was never there; he never sent any cards or letters or made any phone calls. He chose sitting on a bar stool over being with his family. He wanted to drink more than knowing and spending time with me. Not that I expected any presents for my birthday or holidays, but it would have been nice to know he was thinking of us, just a little bit. I didn't expect him to even remember my birthday, but correct me if I'm wrong, but don't the bars celebrate Christmas too?

As I told you before, he used to come and pick us up for a day every now and then until I was around 4 years old. I remember him taking us to his brother's house. My sister and I spent our time following some kids we were told were our cousins around. I remember him playing pool in their basement and smoking cigarettes.

I remember riding with him in his car and laughing as he drove fast over the hills that gave me that funny feeling in my stomach. There is another memory of going to visit him in a small camper he stayed in. After our visits were cut out, he never made any attempt to visit us at all after that. Anyway, he didn't come by to pick us up or to drop off any more presents.

Once when I was around seven, I do remember seeing him. My sister and I went on a camping trip with one of our cousins. He came by when we were getting ready to leave. I don't remember him speaking to us other than to say, "Hi." I remember how he looked. His face was thin and he looked pretty gaunt. I don't recall feeling anything only wondering who this man was.

I saw him once again I believe when I was around 14 years old. By this time my memories of him were pretty blurry and I really didn't care who he even was. The next time I seen him in person was at his brother's wake. My "Uncle" had died from cancer. He was an alcoholic and a pretty ornery one that that. Mom used to be good friends with his wife until the divorce, but afterwards, she was not allowed to speak to Mom. I guess that lady feared her husband more than she wanted to talk to mom, so that's how it was.

When he passed, Mom wanted to make a showing at his wake but didn't want to go alone. She wanted to show the family she survived even without their help. I was pregnant with my second child at this time. My husband went with us to be there for me. Maybe I should tell the truth. I made him go.

Well, I depended on my husband for support when I was scared and unsure of what I was doing. All I really had to do was ask him to go. He knew if he didn't and I was hurt, he would never forgive himself. It really boiled down to him loving me and wanting to be there to protect me from everyone and everything. Lord knows I needed it then.

I remember watching Mom's ex-husband walk into the funeral parlor. My husband was near him at the time and heard him ask his relatives "Who is that lady and young gal?" His other brother laughed and asked what the matter was? Didn't he recognize his ex-wife and daughter when he seen them? My husband took me aside and told me what he heard. He felt I should know my own father didn't recognize me. When I had about all I could take of the stares and finger pointing, I excused myself from my mother's side telling her I needed to go get a Dew. (Short for Mountain Dew)

When I went outside to find the pop machine I had passed earlier, he was standing beside it having a smoke. The one guy I walked out of my way to avoid and dumb me walked right to him. He said hi and asked how I was. I was polite and answered him. My husband came out to look for me and ended up talking with him as well.

The old man tried to explain to me what he had been doing all these years. He didn't know how many times he thought of stopping in to see me when he was in town. I just smiled and nodded my head. I didn't know who he thought he was fooling. Maybe he was trying to fool himself because he sure wasn't me.

He even asked if he could stop by my house to see me and my daughter once in a while. I said I didn't mind if he did. I figured, what the heck. Besides, he didn't stop in all these years, what would make him come now? After a bit, I told him I needed to get back with my mother, said it was nice talking with him and walked away.

Later I found out, that after I excused myself, my husband talked to him a while longer. He told him he was welcome in our home as long as he was not drinking. He was not to even think about stopping if he had anything to drink at all. He did call me shortly after that time to let me know he was in town and to ask if he could come see me and my girls.

I went a mite crazy flying around the house making sure everything was clean and as perfect as I could make it. Not that I wanted to impress him, it was just that it scared me to death and I needed something to do to keep me from going crazy. Not that it mattered. He never showed up.

After mom found out he called me and I gave him

permission to come to my house, it was a whole new story. She became very angry with me and said things I'd like to think she really didn't mean. Bottom line was I couldn't blame her. She spent all that time trying to build a life that was free of him and his problems and there I was letting it all back in again.

That wasn't the way I saw it. I just didn't feel saying "No, don't come see me and your grandchildren." was proper. Even though he was a drunk and chose his life, I felt he still had the right to say he made a mistake and to try to make amends. I think a little part of me wanted to show him that I made a good life for myself without his help even if he chose to be there or not, I really did not need him. I think it was a mixture of all those things and I had hoped after mom calmed down a mite, she would see that. I'm not sure she ever did, but in time, it passed and she forgave me, I think. As with all the rough times of my life, I survived.

After mom's divorce was final, she began dating her original boyfriend; the man she Dear-Johned all those years ago. They just seemed to pick up where they left off. In the early years, I don't remember many fights between them. It wasn't long after they began dating again, they were known around town as a couple. Her boyfriend worked for the city and everyone seemed to know him. I'm not sure if he was well liked, but everywhere we went, someone always said hi and struck up a conversation.

They spoke many times of getting married. I remember them talking and they would plan a house they would build for the four of us. Mom would probably sell her house and we would add on to his house and remodel it. I remember sitting at the kitchen table looking at the plans and asking which room was going to be my room. I would dream of living there. It seemed like it would be real, but nothing ever came of it. They would plan, they would fight, they would make up, they would plan, they would fight...well you get the idea.

They never married. They are still pretty close; although I know he irritates my mother. I think it is a love-hate relationship. They both love to be there to drive each other crazy. I know the feelings are there deep down for each other but I guess things have worked out for the best. They both still have their own freedom with no legal ties.

I have to say that growing up; he was the only father I knew. Good or bad, he is what I had. I idolized him. I was happy to see him and to play cards or any game he wanted to play at the time. He was old school and was a full-blooded Italian. Not that this is a bad thing, it is just that he is probably one of the most stubborn men I have ever known. Explaining anything to him is out of the question. When he gets something in his head, then that is what it is. Don't get me wrong. He helped out my mother a lot. He was there for her when she needed him. But he took a lot too.

I remember the fights. The times I didn't like was when they were fighting, she'd lock the door to keep him out. He'd be on the other side hollering to be let in. She'd yell at him to go home and leave her alone. He'd beg my sister and me to open the door for him. I'd always look at my mom and she'd warn me to not open that door for him. I was always torn. I wanted to please both of them, but I just didn't like the fighting or the hollering.

One time he came over to the house drunk as a skunk. I remember her getting mad and telling him to leave. He said he had to go to the bathroom. After a bit, I remember hearing the biggest thunk I have heard. I ran to the bathroom because it was all quiet. After opening the door real slow like, I saw him. He fell backwards and was cross wise into the tub.

As he sat there, he just looked all confused as to how he got there. He saw me and told me to help him because he couldn't get out of the tub on his own. His legs were sticking out of the tub and he was just plain stuck. I had to get my sister because alone, I was not strong enough to pull him up. We pulled him up together and mom got mad again and ordered him out of the house. It was a few days before he came back after that one.

I remember we'd plan on going somewhere and then not being able to go because he didn't show up to take us. If there was an argument before we were to go, he wouldn't come over. I wasn't sure why at the time, but I think now it was to show my mom how much she needed him to do things and to go places. He never wanted her to have a decent car to depend on because he wanted her to depend on him. Mom hated that. I remember finding my mom sitting at our kitchen table crying. She would never say why when I asked her what was wrong, but I remember her tears.

I have nothing but respect for what he did for us and how he helped. In my heart there will always be a soft spot for the man I used to believe him to be. But

I also remember the pain he caused. I just have to keep in mind it was not my place to change this for her, but just to be there for her if she ever needs to talk and to lend a shoulder. What is done is done. Life moves on. We do survive.

Chapter 5

My second pet came to me about this time. It was again a cat. It was a stray I had found on my way home from the pool one day. Some other kids were being mean to it and I didn't like it. I took it and said, "It's going with me." I knew I shouldn't have done that; mom would be mad at me. But I couldn't leave it either.

When I got home, thankfully, mom wasn't home from work. I took the kitten into the house and gave it a bath because it looked really dirty. I cleaned it up and tried to kill all the fleas it had. I dried it off and fed it some milk and went to wait outside our back door.

I was holding him when she walked up to the house. Right away, she said no, but I told her if she let me keep it, I would keep it in the garage and I would take good care of it. Promising to never bring it in the house, I told her how I found it and I felt sorry for it and knew it needed a home. She gave in but reminded me of the part where it was to stay in the garage. I was overjoyed. I immediately fixed a bed for it in the garage and fed it again. I got cat food the next day, and I was happy.

The cat stayed in the garage until one really cold

night. I didn't say anything to mom about it, but I worried about the poor cat. As night fell, mom was the one who said to me, "You best bring that cat in the back porch so it doesn't freeze to death out there." I brought him in like she told me to. After all, I had to listen to her, right? Didn't want to be getting into any trouble for not listening to what I was told. Kind of funny how things just work out isn't it.

Really, I could have grown up in worse circumstances. I learned a lot from my mom. The lessons she taught was how to be strong, to be self-reliant. She taught me that it didn't matter what you had; it was how you took care of it that counted. It was taking pride in and being true to yourself. It took me a while to realize I even knew all of this. But that was before I got my "adult brain". Through the years, I have come to realize a lot. I know what to value. I know what love is. Yes, I know you don't believe me, but I do. Maybe later I will clue you in, but for now, just know it took me many years to learn all this.

Matter of fact, there are several things I refuse to talk about in mixed company. The first two are the norm; politics and religion. No matter how hard I try, I can't get into a decent conversation about these two. It is always one's point of view above another. One is right and one is wrong and the debate begins on which is which, only it gets loud and angry.

Believe me, this is a never ending, rocky path that should not be taken lightly. I feel it is just best not to go down it; saves a lot of time and frustration. The third is what happens behind closed doors in the bedroom area. Some things should remain there and all too often one feels like they should be bragging or describing everything. Some things are private and intimate and should only be shared between two people, period.

Mom wanted us to grow up different than she did. She grew up very poor with not much of anything. I remember we had a lot of toys, maybe not what was a lot for some, but it seemed like a lot for us. Mom had a terrible fear of drowning, so she hated water. Not so she wouldn't take a bath or anything, but she feared pools and hated when water was poured over her head. She told me she almost drowned in a horse tank when she was a kid. I guess she was playing and from I remember, she was either pushed in or she fell, but she came close to drowning. She didn't want us to have the same fear, so as soon as she figured we were old enough to learn to swim, she had us take swimming lessons.

I'm not sure she even knew, but I remember almost drowning myself one day. The place where we took the lessons was at a private house. The lady taught other kids to swim as she had her own pool on her property. There were other kids also taking lessons, so she must have made good money doing it. I remember being held and shown how to swim. We practiced the dog paddle and how to hold our breath. We were told not to go in the deep end until we learned to swim better. I remember holding on to the side of the pool and inching my way into the deeper water. I don't know exactly why I did this, but I do remember doing it.

I lost my grip on the side of the pool and could not regain it. As I went under water, I would struggle to get back above water. I don't remember choking or breathing in any water. Holding my breath was not the problem, I just could not grab the side of the pool.

Each time I got myself up I'd grab for the side and slip off again. After four or five times, the teacher finally noticed me and ran to grab my hand. She chewed me out for not going under to the bottom and bouncing to where I could stand. I guess that don't enter a person's mind when you're in that kind of trouble. All I thought was, I really need to get a hold of that side to pull myself up. Funny thing was, it didn't make me fear water at all.

I'm not sure if she ever told my mom though. Maybe she was afraid of losing our business, or maybe she didn't want it known she almost lost one of her kids. I have no idea, but I don't remember telling mom either. Maybe I was afraid she wouldn't let me swim anymore because I really loved the water. It just never occurred to me that I should tell her.

After that, I think mom found out it was cheaper to let us kids take swimming lessons from the public pool, because it became a summer ritual after that. The public pool opened like the day or so after school ended and stayed open until the fall when school started back up again. Our lesson would be only in the first few weeks of the pool opening, so we got to go from around 10 in the morning until noon. We would go back home and then be back at the pool when it opened at 1 pm.

Days when it was normal, we'd get up between eight and 9 am and rush through our many lists of chores mom left for us. We knew if we went to the pool and did not have our chores done; there would be heck to pay. We'd be sure we got them done so we could be down to the pool waiting when the doors opened at 1 pm. We stayed until 5 pm when it closed and was back again as it was open again from 7 pm to 9 pm. It was what we did everyday unless it rained.

As I spent each day in the water, I used to tan dark like every girl wanted to. I remember my sister just never could sport a good tan. It was not from the lack of trying either. I remember she'd buy every kind of tanning cream there was. It was just smelly lotion to me as I never had any use for it. I remember we'd both walk or ride our bikes to the pool together, but that was where our togetherness ended. She'd go with her friends and lie on beach towels near the side of the pool. I'd go meet up with my friends and play in the water. My sister and her friends would spend hours doing nothing but lay in all positions on their towels and goop that stuff all over. I tried it once, but got bored really quick and decided swimming in the water with my friends was a lot more fun.

Every now and then, I'd love to tease her by getting out of the pool just to drip water on her. After getting her mad, I'd run and jump back in the pool, laughing my backside off. She'd never follow me because she didn't want to get her hair wet. I never understood this because after all, were we not at the pool? Were we not supposed to get wet? Anyway, I'd always show her my tan line and ask her how her tan was. She'd get mad at me and tell me to shut up because she never tanned at all. She would burn red, but then after peeling, she'd be white again.

I never really cared how tan I was, but it was usually pretty dark and all I knew is it made her mad to see it. She'd try to get me in trouble by telling mom that I got her wet at the pool and she was mad about it. That was pretty ridiculous and mom couldn't get mad at me for that. Most kids went to the pool to swim and get wet. It wasn't long before she'd just ignore her complaints about that.

I learned to swim pretty good and always had a good time at the pool. I never wanted to go home and couldn't wait to be at the pool every day. Mom would never come to swim with us but maybe once that I remember because of her fear. She wouldn't get very wet and she wouldn't go past the 3-foot area. Most times, she'd come out and sit and watched us swim. I know that couldn't have been too exciting, but I think she was very glad to see we didn't have her fear of water.

I knew I was different from the other kids. The things they used to do easily was difficult for me. My legs just didn't move as fast as I wanted when I ran with the other kids. I wasn't as strong as they were and I even walked differently than they did. In time, we found out I was born with a rare bone disease. It never bothered me to know I had it; I just knew it caused a lot of pain. I remember when we first found out I had it.

My sister was big into gymnastics. Nothing professional, just a normal kid practicing things like flips, cartwheels and the splits at home. We weren't supposed to do stuff like that inside, but I remember her flipping over the arm of our chair when mom wasn't home. Little sister wanted to be like big sister, so whatever she did, I tried to do. After her flipping over the chair, I told her I could too and I tried. Only my arm was not strong enough to support me and crumpled under my weight. I didn't break it, but I remember it hurt like the dickens. It swelled up and mom was concerned when she came home and saw it.

She took me to the doctor and I had x-rays. The doctor couldn't tell her what it was, but he was sure I'd grow out of it in time. Mom wasn't so sure and really wanted to find out what it was. The doctor became angry and threw a list of specialists' names at her. He told her she could waste her money on these doctors if she really wanted to.

I remember going to this special doctor for a while and then learning I needed surgery to keep the use of my right arm. One bone had quit growing and the other had bowed. If it kept on like that, I'd lose the use completely because of the way it was growing. He assured her I'd keep the use after he "fixed" it but I would need to be watched. The surgery was pretty scary, but I got through it.

I had a cast on my right arm for about 9 weeks as it healed. It was always weaker and I had to always be careful with it after that. Mom worried constantly and told me I should be easy on it. I was afraid of hurting it more, but I soon realized it just wasn't worth worrying about. It was what it was and I had to deal with the pain no matter how I treated it. I soon learned how to handle it and got on with my life.

One other thing she let me do in the 7th grade was play basketball. This always amazed me because she was pretty protective of what I did since my surgery. I would ask her if I could do something, I thought was cool and she'd always said no, she was afraid I'd fall and break my arm. That's the answer I got when I asked if I could have a skateboard. It was definitely out of the question.

I'd a thought basketball was in that same category. I was amazed the day I came home from school and asked if I could join the school team and she actually said yes. My cousin asked if I would join because they needed bodies for the team. I know she didn't ask because she thought I was good because I was pretty awkward. I could dribble the ball and that's about it.

Like anything else I did, the more I practiced, the better I got. I still wasn't fast, but because of my height, they made me a backup guard. I played for a while, but did have some troubles. I remember in the middle of a game one night, and when I caught the ball, I caught it weird and jammed my middle finger. I tried to tell the coach about it, but got ignored and was told to keep playing. It was sore for a while until I popped it back. I remember how it felt and always tried to avoid it in the future.

One gal who was a year older than me was always on me about my skills. One day stuck out in my memory. We were doing this exercise that helped us with our throwing and catching. The coach wanted us to practice our passing skills so we formed this circle. We had a number of balls and had to throw them back and forth. This gal threw the ball so hard at me that when I caught it, my finger jammed. I complained because I knew I had my fingers bent like I was supposed to when I caught it, but it still jammed anyway. The coach just told me not to be a baby and I was to keep going. It hurt so badly, and I was stubborn enough to keep going.

I had my finger taped for a couple of months because it wouldn't seem to heal. I ended up by jamming it again and actually fixing it. I was really surprised and wished I had done that sooner because the pain went right away. It sure would have saved me a lot of pain because just doing the many things we had to for practice hurt something fierce. The next time that girl threw the ball at me; I would step out of the way.

She'd yell at me and tell me to catch it. I knew I could have, but I was afraid of jamming my fingers again. Since I had a weak right arm, I always had it wrapped to try to help protect it when I played. I made the mistake of telling the coach she best wrap it because I almost forgot to have it done. It was something I needed done, not something I thought of constantly because I hurt less when I didn't pay attention to it. That's how I learned to deal with all the pain I always felt. I got pretty good at putting pain out of my mind to try to diminish it. The only time I can't do that is when I have a headache.

One of the other girls heard me and said pretty mean, "If you forgot, maybe you don't need it." People never paid much attention to me and just didn't know I had the bone disease. They didn't realize what it took for me to do what I did because of the pain I always felt. I had to work three times harder than anyone else to do the same things they took for granted. They didn't care to know and they didn't want to take the time to find out. It was like suffering in silence because no one listened and no one cared.

I played basketball for about three years until I decided to quit. I got a part time job after school and mom told me I could quit because she felt making money was more important than playing a game. I did miss being on the team though. We weren't very good and actually, we hardly ever won a game, but I did like playing. I felt like it helped to keep me in shape with all the running and moving I had to do.

It wasn't like I got much attention playing because since I really wasn't very good, I never started any game and only played to give the others a rest. Whenever I did play, I always tried my best. They never seemed to want me to try to get a score, but it didn't stop me from trying. I remember running down the court and having the time tick down. I was only really allowed to play when the time was almost gone anyway.

I figured, what the heck, I might as well try. One time in particular, I remember trying and actually hitting the hoop. The ball rolled around the hoop and got stuck on the metal part that attached the hoop to the backboard. It stopped the whole game. Everyone laughed and someone took a picture of it. It was pretty funny, but it sucked because I didn't get the credit for the score. I guess it is the story of my life. Trying hard, almost making it and not getting credit for it.

I guess before I get off track again, I should keep telling you of the day. Just poke me when I start to get sidetracked, because I tend to do that very easily. Anyway, back to that fateful day.

Chapter 6

Since I started high school, I wanted to become a veterinarian. Before that it was many different things. I wanted to be a doctor, a teacher, a policeman and even a truck driver. I guess I was pretty confused as a child. I don't think I was different than any other kid in that respect. My ideas and wants seemed to change with the weather.

The first time I realized I had to quit confiding in my mom about what I liked or wanted was one Sunday after church. There was a man who was the nephew of mom's boyfriend. He was the spitting image of him; they looked so much alike; it was scary. The only difference was, one was older and one was younger. I whispered to mom one day after watching him in church that I thought he was very handsome.

Later that morning when we were at her boyfriends for breakfast, she laughed and told him what I said soon after he walked in the room. She seemed to think it was so cute, but I was mortified. The thing that hit me was I told her a confidence. Something I didn't want anyone else to know. She showed me at a pretty young age, I could not trust her.

Later when I confided in her about things, I felt

like I wanted to do with my life, she would tell me to grow up and not be so silly. She would tell me there is no way I could ever do that and I should look to a more practical idea. It was a hard lesson to learn, but I learned it well. I learned I could not talk to my mother; I just couldn't tell her my dreams or my wishes or even speak my deepest and darkest secrets. I couldn't be truly honest with her least I be condemned to being stupid my entire life.

Before beginning high school and after being told many times I would have to soon decide what I wanted to do with my life, I finally decided on a path. I decided to form my life around the animals I loved. If it were possible, I was going to be a veterinarian. I looked into what credits I would need and geared my whole high school experience toward that goal. I found out I needed all the science courses. I was a mite worried about passing chemistry and shook at the thought of trying to pass physics. I will proudly report that I made it through both classes with a high B.

By the time I was a junior in high school, I figured everything was set. I had the required courses and worked long and hard to achieve it. I felt suffering through those few years would be worth what I was to gain in my future. I had a little bit of money saved in the bank. I had my school picked out. Everything was mapped and in the bag. I knew where I was going. I knew what I was going to do. I sat back to have a breeze senior year.

As a senior, I wouldn't need any English courses. Since English was my worst subject, I was very happy with this. Back then, Spanish counted as an English course, so as a freshman, I took Spanish to get out of taking English my senior year. It worked out to my advantage quite well. My hardest class during my last year of high school would be physics. This class for me would be sheer heck.

To make matters worse, my schedule had the class the very first hour of the day. I knew I couldn't be late or skip or else I would be totally lost in the class. It was like going from sleeping in a very comfortable bed to sitting on a hard bench listening to radio fuzz! As worried as I was, I knew I could handle one hard course with the rest being easy.

Yep, I thought I had planned it all out; I thought I had it made; until that day. That fateful day, my world turned upside down and inside out; the day that changed my whole life. Funny thing was, it changed real quiet like, without me knowing it. Like it crept up on me and kicked me in the backside. I guess the excitement of finally having my own bass lulled me into thinking my changes were done for a while. I was really wrong.

After I came home with my new baby (my bass guitar, don't go thinking I was in trouble yet), I was proud as a peacock. I would spend hours playing then polishing the bass marveling at its beauty. I was beginning to get a mite nervous because that following Wednesday would be the day when I tried playing in a real band. I couldn't seem to sit still. I knew I wouldn't last because I couldn't play by ear. I had no clue of how to even do this as I always played by sheet music and I had never heard of country bands having sheet music when they played. I knew I was sunk before I even tried. But try I did.

I borrowed an amplifier from my so-called boyfriend I had at the time because me owning one was not in the deal I had made with my mom. I guess I didn't plan that part out quite right. This boyfriend was not really for me, but I didn't know it then. We just went out on a mutual understanding. He never really asked me to go steady, we just dated. Mom actually liked him, so it wasn't a problem with her.

There were times when he stood me up because he was dating another girl and then would call me expecting me to drop what I was doing for him. I just got tired of waiting around and I didn't figure this to last long because it always made me angry. I didn't like the fact that I didn't even deserve a simple phone call from him, yet I was supposed to be at his beck and call. Just didn't seem like a proper trade off. At the time, he did let me use his amplifier when I asked for it, so for the time being, I let things go and was happy.

I remember driving up to the Kempo shop where the practice was supposed to take place and walking in. I left my equipment in the car because I wanted to find out how far I had to carry it. As I walked in and looked around, my heart dropped and did flip flops. Instant fear went through my whole body. This guy that sat on the bench looking through a magazine was the cause of these dreaded feelings. I knew this guy from high school. I remembered him. He was a senior when I was a freshman. I could not believe it was him. My mind started racing with old memories. I remember thinking, "Oh no...anyone but him!"

This guy was probably the biggest and toughest boy everyone in school feared. When I was a freshman, the seniors used to pick on me. Now I'm not talking the joking kind where someone kids you and you return it for fun. I'm talking the mean, put down, going to make you cry type of picking on. It got to be so bad, that I even stopped eating lunch in the cafeteria at school because I couldn't take it anymore. It was these senior's favorite thing to do.

They would sit near the place where you had to return lunch trays and make fun of you. It was horrible to hear what they had to say and to listen to them laugh. If you tried to stand up for yourself, it made things worse as everyone would start to gang up on you. You usually ended up by getting out of there as quick as you could. You hoped you wouldn't be seen, but they always did and all you could do was pray you didn't trip as you walked as fast as you could without running.

Like I said before, my self-confidence was pretty low. Some folks still say it still is low today, but I'm not all sure about that. You see my defenses I created back then got to be pretty good. Since I didn't have the body strength to fight anyone, I decided I had to out think them. It was mind over body so to speak. I figured if I agreed with them, then there would be no argument and they'd leave me alone. It usually worked out pretty well. I still avoided them whenever I could, but if I met up with them, my defenses kicked in.

I remember walking down the hall and I would hear some kid say, "Gee isn't she ugly!" I would turn and say, "Yep you sure are right!" They usually didn't know what to say with me agreeing with them, so they would leave me alone right quick. They'd give me a strange look as if they couldn't think of a comeback and usually end up by either walking away or just ignoring me and not saying anymore. I guess somewhere along the line I just started to believe it. It was very easy to do. Sometimes know I do go too far, but hey, habit is habit.

Anyway, as much as I feared the seniors, I feared this Big Guy the most. Even the seniors that teased me and made my life heck, feared him I think worse than I did. He wasn't all that huge, but he had facial hair that seemed to make him look mean. He had a look in his eye that said "I can beat the tar outa you without even trying." I knew he was tough when even the seniors who picked on me got quickly out of his way as fast as they did.

In school, when I walked down the halls, I walked so close to the walls and was so quiet, I could blend in with the paint. You never knew I was there. When he walked down the halls, it was like Moses parting the Red Sea. Everyone moved out of his way and I do mean everyone moved so he could walk down the dead center of the hall. He didn't even have to say, "Move or I'll tear your head off!" They just plain moved after a quick look from him. He had quite the reputation for fighting. Not too many wanted to tangle with him. I heard he never lost a fight, ever.

One day, I remember walking through the hall and even bumped right into him. I was looking down, so I didn't even see him walk up to me. I looked up to see who I almost ran into and saw him. My heart froze. He smiled and said "Hi!" to me. I was so scared. I said hi and bolted down the hall as quick as I could. I had no clue what he wanted and there was no way in God's green earth that I was going to stick around and see what he wanted either. Yes, I ran. Quick as my chubby legs could take me, I tell you. Fear does that to a person.

When I walked through that door that night of my first real band practice and seen him sitting there, I had nowhere to run. He looked up and smiled at me. He looked at me with those bright baby blue eyes that seemed to melt my heart and asked if I needed help with my equipment. He did one thing that rankled me and brought me back to the present. He called me kid. This sort of ticked me off, because I felt that at my age, I was no kid! I didn't exactly figure myself to be a woman either, but kid certainly did not cut it. So, my anger helped me to clear my head and stay without running away as quick as I had before. Looked like I had something to prove.

He did help carry my equipment in and waited while I set it up. I kept looking at him and wondering what he was thinking because he kept looking at me with those blue eyes. Why hadn't I noticed those eyes before? I guess I was too scared and nervous to see them. I just kept looking back at him and smiling and wondering when either of them would say, "Yep, you're terrible like you said, you can go now."

Before we even started to play, I told them again I could not play by ear. I started to bring up the sheet music thing again, but the Big Guy just smiled and said to relax, that everything would be okay. I tried, but I really was not so sure. The first song they tried to teach me was Country Roads by John Denver. I totally messed it up; killed it deader than a door nail. I couldn't keep up and I couldn't play the right notes to save my soul. Every now and then, I did hit the right one, but as soon as I did, I would be behind again. It seemed to take forever until the song was over. I just wanted to curl up and die from embarrassment because I was playing so terrible.

I remember looking at the Big Guy and smiling trying to ask for forgiveness with my eyes for being such a terrible bass player. After all, I did tell them. There should have been no surprises. He didn't seem to care that night. I couldn't get over how he just talked to me and encouraged me to keep playing. I know he tried to make me feel better, but I didn't. I could have kicked myself in the backside for being so horrible. If it were me, I'd a showed myself the door and told myself to sell that poor bass and never play again! With time, I eventually got better, but even today, I still have a tough time playing that song. Like through everything else I have been through, I have survived; even that embarrassment.

I was a terrible bass player. I knew it. What I didn't know was why they kept me. I expected at any moment for one of them to say, "Okay, you're done, you can go, you're terrible!" I found out later after that first fateful night, my Kempo instructor wanted to dump me right away, but the Big Guy wouldn't let him. The Big Guy told me he saw it as a great opportunity to teach me to play like he wanted so we could have our own unique sound. That one reason kept me besides the fact that the Big Guy liked me. I was really surprised to find this out. I didn't think anyone could like me.

We often talk about the past. I have since found out what he wanted that fearful day back in high school. That day I bumped into him and ran away. He was going to ask me to go with him to the Homecoming dance. After I ran, he just thought I was stuck up. As he watched me run away, he asked his friend what he thought of me. The friend said "She is cute, but she is a bit stuck up, isn't she?" He didn't like stuck up people. So, he never tried to ask me out again.

I also found out why he fought so much. When he was in grade school and middle school, he was not very big. He weighed less than 95 pounds soaking wet. Like me, he got picked on too. I found out when a boy picks on a girl mean like, it is with words. When a boy picks on another boy mean, it is way worse. The talking is usually done with fists. There were kids that would gang up on him and beat him up and even chase him around. I'm not sure how I would have handled violence like that.

It kept up and was pretty normal for him until one day after Christmas. His mom had given him a snorkel coat for a Christmas present. It was pretty expensive and was the fad back then. You older guys and gals may remember these coats. They were the winter coats that zipped all the way up the hood and made the hood look like a dog head or like you were snorkeling, hence the name, snorkel coat. Anyway, his mom bought him one for Christmas.

He came from a big family and it was not a "right" family name either. They didn't have a lot of money and really treasured when they could buy something like that. He wanted to wear his new coat to school and his mom told him not to, that some kid would ruin it for him. He told his mom that it would be okay and he would take care of it and wore it to school anyway. As he was walking through the hall, one kid, the biggest and the meanest bully of them all came up to him. He ripped the sleeve completely off the coat.

Let me tell you what happened next. The Big Guy (he wasn't so very big at this time) saw red. He knew he was in for a beating from his mom when he got home for not listening to her about wearing the coat to school. It made him boiling mad cause he was very proud of the coat. He had wanted one for so long and now that he had it, another ruined it for no good reason. He just went crazy. He started beating this bully. Now this bully was a state wrestler and was pushing 300 pounds. At the time, the Big Guy was barely 95 pounds soaking wet.

When he went nuts, all he could think about was beating this bully to death. He made the bully bleed out his eyes, ears, nose and mouth. It took about five male teachers to pull the Big Guy off the bully. And when they would pull him off, he would somehow wiggle loose from their grip and continue to beat him. They did finally call an ambulance to take the kid to the hospital. The Big Guy got into trouble over this one. I'm not sure how many detentions he had to serve, but I do know he got called from the middle school to the high school office because the mother of this bully wanted to see the "big bad bully" that beat up her precious son.

When he got to the office and checked in with the receptionist, the bully and his mother was there too. The bully looked at him once and then put his head down and would not look up again. The Big Guy sat down next to his mother and waited. She finally asked the receptionist when this "bully" was going to get here. The receptionist said, "Well, he is sitting right there." The mother turned to look at the Big Guy and said, "No way!! This little kid could not have been the one that beat up my son." The Big Guy admitted to her as to being the one who did it and she asked why would he do a thing like that.

Since she asked, he told her. He told her everything. Of how her precious son bullied everyone in the whole school. Of how everyone in school is scared of him. He told her of how her son would seek him out to beat him up every day and how it was the last straw when her son pulled the sleeve off of his brand-new coat. He said he did feel bad he hurt him like he did, but her son had it coming. She turned to her son and asked him if all this was true. All her son would do is sit there, look at his feet and nodded. She got angry and cuffed him on side his head and told him to get back to his class. The Big Guy sat there while she talked with the principle. He was allowed to go back to his classes as well.

He thought he was pretty much off the hook until he walked home and saw the mother's car parked outside his house. His heart sunk as he walked up to his front door. He hadn't told his mom about any of this and hoped the school wouldn't call either. He knew he was in for it now no matter what happened.

He walked in the house and got greeted by his mother at the door. The mother of the bully was sitting there in a chair just waiting. His mother asked him if there was anything, he wanted to tell her about. He said, "Yea mom, I sort of got into a fight at school." Personally, I do believe she was upset with him for not being honest and for not telling her about the whole thing. The bully's mother handed him a box, which contained a new coat. She apologized for her son and hoped there wouldn't be any hard feelings.

The Big Guy did get grounded for all this. His mom told his dad he got in a fight and his dad was mad at the news of the torn coat. He lightened up a mite when he found out about the new coat. He asked the Big Guy, "Well, did you win?" The Big Guy said, "Yea, I guess so; they took the other kid away in an ambulance." His dad just couldn't believe his son beat up a big state champion wrestler. Just goes to show what a person can do when the adrenaline gets a pumping.

After that, the Big Guy found he didn't have to run from anyone anymore. The news spread like wildfire throughout the school. The Big Guy beat the tar out of the school bully. The other kids gave him a respect because the "bully" they all feared was not as scary as he was before. After that, there seemed to be guys who thought they were tough and could take the Big Guy. Turns out, they never could. I found out most of his fights came about because he seen others picking on weaker kids. He'd step up and tell them to leave them be or else. Sometimes I wonder just where he was when I was getting picked on by those same kids, but that is beside the point.

Another reason for his fights was the fact that he just didn't take any guff from anyone. If some guy started to talk smack to him or say something he didn't like, he would usually tell him to knock it off or just clean his clock. He couldn't stand a bully or a smart you know what. I guess there were a lot of different reasons for his fights. Bottom line was, he never started a fight, but he sure finished them.

In spending more and more time with the Big Guy, the more I found out about myself. It was so strange to find someone who thought so much of me. He would tell me things I couldn't believe. He told me he watched me grow up. He always noticed me where ever I was. At least he noticed me and he admitted he probably fell in love with me on that first day he ran into me.

Remember I told you about getting run over by that boy. Well, that boy was him. Was I ever surprised! The more we talked, the more I remembered, the more that made sense. He said he would watch me after that day and think of how cute I was. Yes, I know. I would gag every time he said this. There is no way I ever could think of myself as cute. I just had a tough time believing what he was saying. You know, now that I think on it, it is true a person does have more than one day that changes their life. Maybe everyone's life is filled with a bunch of these days. It's just that we don't know it or don't recognize it when it happens.

The more time we spent together, the closer we became. The more I saw him, the more I realized we were becoming best friends. There was really nothing sexual between us at first. I really was not ready for that. I had my life planned. I did not know myself let alone want to know another person. I did not know I was capable of the love he was maybe looking for. I didn't think anyone would ever want to love me like that anyway. I was happy with just being friends. Best friends.

He was the first person to care about what I thought. When he asked what I was thinking about, he would look into my eyes and wait for me to answer. When I didn't, he would probe for the real answer. Like he knew I was afraid to say. He seemed to know I was afraid to be laughed at. He would ask me what I really wanted. I didn't have to lie or to make up anything; all I had to do was be me. He actually cared about how I felt.

I realized he was the first person to look at me for me. He didn't care what my last name was nor cared if I was carrying around a huge dollar sign or not. It didn't matter to him what people thought of me or what I was supposed to be, he just cared about what I was. He didn't listen to any rumor or any talk. He looked at me, not through me. If he had a question, he asked.

We talked about everything. You have to remember I was still supposed to have been dating this other guy. The Big Guy seemed to know how I was feeling by just looking at me. If I was happy, he would laugh. If I was sad or upset, he'd ask me what was wrong and listen to me without judging while I talked about it. It was unbelievable. I was becoming happy and feeling safe and comfortable. He knew how to make me laugh. He knew when to give me his shoulder. He knew when to let me cry. I felt comfortable and safe and warm when I was with him.

I always felt cold and my hands were freezing most times. It never mattered if I wore gloves or not. He would take my hands and either warm them with his own, or put them inside his coat or pocket. I could never get over how warm he was all the time. He would always smile and tell me cold hands, warm heart. I never knew if this was true, but I did know my hands and feet were always cold. He complains about other areas being cold, but I just tell him since he gave me his word about always being with me, it meant it was now his job to warm it all up. No matter what it was or how cold it got.

As we played more and more music together, and spent more and more time together, I realized just how important music was for us. Music is what brought us together, it helped to strengthen our bond and it gave us fuel for our love. Many times, as we would play a song, we would see ourselves in the song. It was like the song was written for us. As we would play, we would look at each other and smile and become one. It is really hard to describe, but that is what happened very slowly, night after night. I'm not sure we knew it was happening, but happened just the same.

One night, he called me to ask if I'd go to the movies with him. Since I already had a date with my boyfriend, I thanked him for asking, but said I couldn't go. I was home getting ready for my date and I waited. And I waited. And I waited some more. My boyfriend had stood me up again. I got mad and said the heck with this and went down to my usual hangout.

I ran into the Big Guy and had a good time anyway. He made me forget my anger. The next couple of days flew and the next time my boyfriend called me, he started to apologize. I stopped him and told him he could have called to let me know he wasn't picking me up if there was to be a next time.

He said some old friends came into town and he got drunk with them and forgot about our date. I told him that was no excuse.

It really riled me. You can give me a lot of excuses, but being drunk carries no weight with me. I told him what ever, but next time I was not going to sit around and wait on him all night ever again. I told him I could have gone to the movies with the Big Guy but I wasted the night waiting for him instead. Boy, then all heck broke loose. He got mad and told me he didn't like me being friends with the Big Guy and I was not to see him anymore.

I guess I saw red at that and told him right off. See, my mom taught me to stand up for what I believed in. I was not to let anyone tell me what to do, who to be friends with or to make me go against what I thought was right. He sure didn't like it when I told him I would be friends with who I wanted. Besides, we were only friends and since I didn't tell him who to be friends with, he didn't have the right to tell me who to be friends with. Not only that, but since our dating wasn't official like, he really didn't have any power over me at all. If he didn't like it, he could hit the road. Yes, I gave it to him with both barrels!

After that, the Big Guy and I spent more and more time together. I wasn't with him to prove a point, only because I liked being with him. I liked the way he made me feel and above all, I was becoming attached. I didn't care what his last name was. It didn't matter there were rumors. I didn't care about whom he dated before me and I certainly didn't care about the fights or what he had done before we became friends. The only thing that mattered was how he treated me and how he made me feel. For the first time in my life, I was becoming happy with who I was and what I was. It was so weird. I didn't want it to end.

Chapter 7

Now you know all about the day my life changed. I sure didn't see it coming. At first things seemed no different. I didn't see it right off. I think I smiled more and was happier, but that was the only telltale signs I could think of. The more I went to Kempo and the more I learned to play music the happier I was.

As I said before, I spent more and more time with the Big Guy. I remember once after a practice on a Saturday afternoon, we were down to the Kempo shop alone. The Big Guy was there watching the place for the instructor because he had somewhere, he needed to go. It was pretty cold out and the wood furnace needed to be kept full.

The Big Guy and I worked out for a bit and spent some time sitting on a mat just talking. It started to get cool. So, the Big Guy went in the furnace room to stock the stove. While I was alone in the workout room, I decided to try to bench press the weights. I laid down on the bench and lifted weights off the rack. I pressed it just fine until I started to giggle. Bad thing was, the more I laughed, the weaker I got. I could not for the life of me lift the weights off my chest to put them back. I was stuck.

I started to really giggle about the predicament I

got myself into. I kept thinking, man, am I silly! I really wished the Big Guy would come back into the room and save me, but he just didn't come back for a long time. I tried to call for him, but I couldn't cause I couldn't quit giggling. He was taking so long to come back, it seemed like he was planting the trees and waiting for them to grow before he burned them.

When he finally came back in the room after what seemed like eons, he saw me stuck under the weights. I'm laughing and trying to tell him, "HELP!!" He walked right up to me and starts laughing saying, "Hmmm, looks like we got us a situation here!" I could finally talk a little, so I told him to shut up and get this dang thing off me! He still laughed and I got a lecture on how dangerous it was for me to lift weights by myself. He made things worse by easily lifting them with one hand and put them back on the rack. It was a pretty embarrassing moment let me tell you!

The days I had my lesson were the days he would come to my Kempo class. Since he was trained in the military, he liked to spar with my teacher, his master and the other guys who also took lessons. It was also time for us to be together so two birds were hit with one stone so to speak. When we would spar together the Big Guy would be very gentle with me.

We'd start sparing and I would really try to get a point on him. It wouldn't be long before he'd get me in a throw and hold me and gently take me down to the mat. He'd hold me there longer than he should and I'd have to say, "Okay, you can let go now!" He'd laugh and let me up and do it all over again. It always disgusted me to know how easy he took me down, but he never hurt me, so it was okay. I didn't mind it so bad. It was actually kind of fun.

The Big Guy taught Judo to the instructor and some of the guys who took lessons. I learned later this was his trade off. He would walk through every guy who tried to fight him. No one was a match for him. I watched one day as the Big Guy even took on my instructor and the master in a sparring match. He fought the both of them at once and held his own. The instructor was a black belt and pretty good, but he didn't have any weight to back up what he did. The Big Guy would blow him away and then fight the Master.

The Master looked like an old guy who had trouble bending and tying his own shoes. That was so far from what he was, it was funny. He was very good at sparring and could actually beat a person by using an opponent's own punches and energy against themselves. He couldn't use this technique against the Big Guy however. The Big Guy was too strong for that. As he would get a point, the Big Guy would get one back and it kept going. It turned out to be a draw until way near the end. The Big Guy finally beat him. It was something to see and the Master was amazed at the Big Guy's skills. He proclaimed the Big Guy to be a natural.

There was one guy who was doomed by his arrogance started with me and was in my class. He was kind of a loud mouth kid and knew just enough to get himself hurt. He had very good form when he performed his katas, but when it came to fighting, he felt like he could take everyone and anyone. A kata was the part of the lesson where we learned the movements as a sort of a dance. It would show strength and coordination and grace.

He wanted so bad to spar against the Big Guy, but it wasn't allowed. The Big Guy always refused to spar with him because number one, he irritated the Big Guy and number two, the Big Guy learned to kill. There was no way this kid could handle the Big Guy only he wouldn't recognize it. Even the master was afraid the Big Guy would kill him if they sparred.

One day this kid asked me to spar and since I welcomed the practice, I agreed. I held my own and after I got a point on him, he reached over and hit me in the back of the head when I wasn't looking. Then he smiled pretty wickedly at the Big Guy. This riled him and the Big Guy finally said, "Okay, now we will fight!"

The instructor tried desperately to stop it, but the Big Guy had his mind set. Hitting me was something he wouldn't stand for and he figured it was time he gave the kid what he was asking. I guess the kid was overjoyed and for the life of me I couldn't figure out why. Couldn't he see the Big Guy was going to kill him?

Apparently, he had gotten it in his head he could take the Big Guy after watching him spar with me. He figured if I could survive it, then he could take the Big Guy. Everyone knew different and they really wanted to watch this match because apparently, he irritated more people than just the Big Guy.

They started fighting and I could tell the Big Guy was toying with him. The kid was dancing around throwing everything he could at him when the Big Guy got tired of playing. His form was pretty good, but it wasn't good enough. I call it the "Splat that was Heard Around the World." The Big Guy put him in a throw and the kid hit the mat so hard he laid there trying to breathe for a long time. He gasped for air and you could hear him sputter, "You didn't have to do that so hard!? We all laughed about it. That kid never bothered me or the Big Guy ever again. Matter of fact he was always quite polite every time we met.

One day I was doing some chores around the house, when the effects of his love first started happening. I was out in the yard, raking the many leaves that always fell when the Big Guy showed up. He started talking to me and asked if I needed help. I was raking and pushing a huge pile of leaves into my burn pile when I stepped out to talk to him better. He looked down and frowned at me and started hitting my pant leg.

Here the bottom fringe of my pants had started on fire and I didn't know it. I was on fire. He said "You're going to burn yourself up if you're not careful!" He seemed angry, but I thought it was funny and started laughing and said, "I guess I kind of made an ash of myself huh?" Well, that got him to smiling and it wasn't long before we were laughing about the whole thing.

He helped me rake the yard and we talked while we worked. We talked a lot about everything and anything. After we finally got the yard raked, we sat down to talk some more. Somehow, his head ended up in my lap and he just kept looking at me with those blue eyes of his. My fingers found their way into his hair and he would just say how much he loved that. He finally said if anything more would happen between us; it would come from me because I was safe with him. He wouldn't start anything. I didn't have to worry about any after with him.

If you're wondering what I mean about the after, you gals should know what I'm talking about. You know, when a fella takes you out, to a movie and to dinner and you have a good time, the after is what is expected when he takes you home. Whether it is a kiss or a hug or more, it's the after that I'm talking about.

Sometimes a gal wants to and sometimes she just wants the fun and is not ready for the after. It all depends on what the guy expects and what he wants. Many a good girl's reputation is ruined due to the after being handled poorly. Either she doesn't want what he wants and he gets mad and makes up rumors, or maybe it's true and things go a little too far and stories get told. I guess it doesn't matter either way, but for a lot of gals, it is something to worry about.

With the Big Guy, he just assured me I didn't have to worry about it. We stayed that way until my old boyfriend showed up and broke the moment. I could tell he didn't like the Big Guy being there like that, but I didn't care. He really didn't seem to want to be with me that bad because he ended up by just leaving. I knew he was mad, but somehow, it just didn't bother me at all. Later, the Big Guy invited me over to his house for his world-famous hot chocolate. Since I really had nothing planned, he walked me to his house and let me tell you that was the best cup of hot chocolate I ever had!

I was so confused in those days. I had no clue

what I really wanted, what I was supposed to do or to feel. Not that long ago, I had everything figured out. I was going to graduate, go on to school, get a good job and have a decent life. No complications, no major decisions to make, no trouble. It was all laid out in front of me. Then all of a sudden, everything changed.

After that day raking the yard and I had such a good time, my mom saw things I didn't see. She kept after me saying, "You best watch it, that Big Guy has a crush on you!" I would tell her; no way and we were just friends. It was nothing to worry about. She didn't seem to believe me, but I didn't care. I thought I knew what I was doing and what I was supposed to do.

As time passed, the Big Guy and I became closer and closer. I was never so happy in my entire life. I was so busy and was always on the run. I kept up the Kempo lessons, kept practicing music with the Big Guy, my studies, events for school and my part time job. The Big Guy started letting me drive his truck to help me save time in walking, so I had to start getting up earlier to be sure he had it while I was in school.

After school, he would pick me up and take me to work and then pick me up after wards. He would either take me home, back to school to play in the pep band, to my Kempo class or to our band practice. I guess thinking back on it now; I was hardly at home during this time. It was no wonder why my mom started to get angry with me. I thought I was keeping a pretty good handle on everything. Even on the weekends, I would stay home to do housework and to help mom out by doing chores I let go during the week.

After I got my job and I earned my driver's license, I'd cash my check each week. Every other week I would put $10.00 in gas in mom's car; keep out 5-10 a week for spending money and save the rest. I didn't have a huge amount of money on me at any time or even a huge amount of money in the bank, but it was enough. I really didn't see there was a problem. When I got my report card, my grades didn't let on as there being a problem either as they had never been better. Pretty much straight A's and I even got a letter saying I was being inducted into the National Honor Society.

Yes, I thought I was doing quite well. I was so happy! To me, I didn't want it to end. And as far as I was concerned, it wasn't going to end. Things were going the way I thought they should be. Of course, we can't see the future can we.

There are a few days that I remember exactly and this is one of them. I remember being very happy; loving the feeling of being carefree with not a worry in my head. I never wanted that to change. I had already spent so much time being unhappy and sad before I met the Big Guy. I was finally happy and I wasn't about to let anything change it or bring me back down ever again. Unfortunately, some things are not meant to be.

I had a couple of friends who I grew up with. They were sisters who lived by me on the next block. They were a year and three years younger than I was and was more like my little sisters than anything. We spent a lot of time playing as kids and were actually through a lot. We had fun and got into trouble together. We would stay at each other's houses, go swimming, and hang out. I remember getting into so much trouble over them more than once.

See, I had my own bike and the rule was, not to let anyone else ride it because we'd be responsible if they fell off and got hurt. It was a pretty strict rule, one I didn't like to break because it would make my mom very angry with me. Since they were younger, I usually did things before they did; I learned to ride a two-wheel bike before either of the two. They begged me to teach them to ride like I could because if they showed their parents they knew how to ride, then maybe their parents would buy them bikes so we could go riding together. They kept saying, "Think of all the fun we could have!"

Well at first, I knew better than to let them try to ride my bike, but they begged and begged me. I told them about my rule. I told them how much trouble I would be in if my mom found out I let them ride my bike. They continued to beg, so I gave in. I made them both promise never to tell my mom about it and we had to do it out of view of my house. I figured as long as I was there to catch them and not let them crash, what was the harm? I wouldn't let them get hurt.

So, I worked with them and taught them both to ride. They did pretty good and was really proud of what they learned. That's where the trouble started. They were so proud they had to run and tell everyone including my mom of what they learned. When she asked them when did their folks buy them a bike of their own, they said they didn't have one that I let them ride mine, and they were soon to get their own. Well, I was in for it. If I remember right, I was grounded for three weeks straight. One week for each girl that rode my bike and one week for defying her. My friends did wait for me to be able to play with them again. It was like a prison sentence.

Was not a good time at my house let me tell you and I was mad at them for a while. But I got over it and it wasn't too long before my mom forgave me and we were riding like a gang up and down our street. We had a lot of fun and went everywhere on our bikes. Anyway, that's who my friends were; two sisters who were neighbors that I considered to be my little sisters.

When we got into school, the other kids didn't see them like I did. I accepted them as they were. Remember the click thing? Well, they were in the same class as I was only, they were way weirder than I was. The oldest sister, who was a year younger than I, was the strangest one. She was born a mite sickly and always seemed to have something wrong with her. She was thin and wore these very strong glasses. She was not very tough and cried about a lot of things I shook off. It was not hard to see why she got made fun of. I would stand up for her a lot of times and tell the other girls to leave her alone. They usually let her alone if they saw me coming.

The younger sister, well, she was something else. She was not sickly and was actually quite healthy. She was a little on the heavy side. Not obese or anything like that, but just hefty. She had a very tender heart and would often blow things out of proportion.

Once, I asked my mom if I could ride my bike up at school around the track. She said I could so I rode my bike up there by myself. I liked to do that because it was mostly the only flat ground you could ride your bike on without worry of having to go up hills to slow you down. You could ride your bike for as long as you wanted with no hills to climb and just feel like you were sailing. I would always let my imagination go and while I was riding, I could be anything I wanted. It was fun and I went up there as often as mom would let me.

Well on this day, I was riding have a great time in my own little world when she came up and stopped me. She told me that my whole family had no clue where I was and was going bonkers trying to find me and man, was I in trouble. I was so scared I had done something wrong, as fear will do to you. I raced home to let them know where I was and that I was okay. I would take whatever punishment I was about to receive.

On the way home, I ran across my sister and frantically told her I was up at the track just riding my bike. Well, she looked at me like I was nuts and said, "So what, I don't care." I asked her if mom was mad at me and why did she want to know where I was? She just told me she had asked my friend in passing where I was and no, mom was not looking for me. Best of all, I was not in trouble.

Man, I had a heart attack for no reason at all. I was a little miffed at her for telling me such lies, but I came to realize that's what she did without meaning to cause trouble. So, at times I never knew when to believe her and when not to pay attention to her. This would later come to bite me right in the backside.

The day I remember started out looking like a good one. I was very happy and didn't have a care in the world. As I said before, things were finally looking up for me. I went to all my classes like normal, but when I got to the band room, something was different. I wasn't sure what it was at first, but I soon figured it out.

In band, I was in the trumpet's first chair's position which sat me right next to the tuba players. The tuba player that sat next to me happened to be my friend I grew up with; the younger sister. During rehearsals, sometimes we would get into a little trouble for laughing when we shouldn't have been. We would sit and talk quietly and make jokes. We always seemed to have a good time. Sometimes we would tease and make fun of her older sister about what weird clothes she was wearing or something weird she had said earlier. We could pick on her, but no one else could. That's the way it was.

This day, was different. She sat in class so quiet. This was so unlike her. She had this sad, faraway look in her eyes. Like she has lost her best friend and she didn't know what to do. Her look struck me and actually stopped me in my thoughts. I asked her to tell me what was wrong and at first, she didn't answer me. After a while, she said nothing was wrong and she was okay, but the look on her face and in her eyes said different.

At the time, I had a feeling in my gut that told me something was wrong, but I was afraid she was blowing something out of proportion and it was nothing really. That's how she was. I had been so happy lately; I didn't want anything to spoil it and to tell the truth, I didn't want to hear anything sad or troubling. I didn't want to be bothered and I didn't want to be brought down. So, I ignored my gut feeling that something was really wrong with her. I didn't pay her any more attention and frankly, I didn't think about it again that day.

The next day, things seemed normal enough. At least I thought so. My friend was not in band which wasn't normal but I didn't think a lot about it. I knew her sister was at school in the morning and I didn't pay attention to see if she was in band that day or not. Nothing out of the ordinary happened that I could see. Before the day was out, her sister's name did get called to go to the office but I didn't think too much about it at the time other than wondering if she was in trouble or not. I left school like normal only I remember I had to walk.

I went home and changed and walked on to work. The day was nice, I really didn't mind walking. I guess there was a strange looking car at my friend's house. I glanced at it but didn't give it much thought. I went to work and heard some whispers and seen some weird looks, but I didn't give that much thought either. I was in my own little happy world.

My supervisor was looking like he wanted to say something. I noticed my friend; the older sister was not at work like she normally was. Finally, my supervisor came up to me and asked if I knew my friend's little sister at all. I said, "Of course I know her, we are best friends," and asked him why he want to know. He just blurted out, "Because she hung herself today. She is dead!"

It was like someone hit me with a baseball bat only I didn't know where the bat came from. I remember him asking me if I was okay. I mumbled I was and he said "Good, get back to work." I went back to my station and just sat there staring at my work. His words were trying to sink in. I could not seem to see what I was looking at. One of my co-workers sitting next to me asked me if I was okay. I said I didn't know because I just found out one of my best friends had died. I started shaking and the tears started flowing.

She took me by the arm and led me into the boss's office. He seen I was in no shape for work and said I could go home. They asked if there was someone I could call to come and get me. I said, "Just my mom." They called home but mom was not there. They asked if there was anyone else, I said, "The Big Guy. He was the only other one I could think of at that moment. I could hardly see to dial his number and hoped it was right as the phone rang. When he answered, I couldn't seem to talk to him much only to ask him to come to pick me up at work.

He picked me up and we just drove. He drove with me through the back roads without saying a thing. He just let me cry. We even had to stop the truck as a huge herd of deer crossed the road in front of us. He pulled me over to his seat and held me. After I composed myself, he said he understood. He had already heard about what had happened. He asked if I wanted to go to my friend's house. I said I guess I best go. We went over there and found out what really happened.

It turned out that my friend indeed had some troubles she was not inclined to talk about. Whatever it was it bothered her something fierce. She went to school and told some of the kids she was going home at noon to commit suicide. They laughed at her and didn't take her serious. Apparently, she was serious. She left school and went back home. For some reason, she didn't do it whether she chickened out or thought better of it, no one really knows. She decided to go back to school.

She ran across those same gals she told about it in the first place. They laughed at her and made fun of her. I hear tell it was pretty bad because it upset her and she left school again. This time she didn't chicken out. From what I was told, she made a tape for her family and took her father's deer rifle down to the basement. She tried to fire it once and then put the barrel under her chin and pulled the trigger.

Isn't it terrible how people start rumors? The rumor had gone around that she had hung herself but that was not the actual truth. I never heard any talk about why she did it, so I can only imagine what they were saying. One of the grapevine ladies even had the nerve to call me and ask about what had happened. I was not in the proper frame of mind, as I did the only mean thing I could think of. I collaborated and repeated the hanging story. I wanted her to tell someone else only to be made a fool of when the real truth was told. I probably shouldn't have, but at the time I didn't care.

After we spent some time with her family, we noticed it had started snowing pretty good outside. My mom was there talking too. I looked at the Big Guy and announced I thought I should go home and shovel the walk so mom could get in the door easier. He agreed that we should and we asked the older sister if she wanted to get out of the house for a while and go with us to shovel. She agreed, so we all walked together to my house.

When we shoveled, we usually ended up in some kind of a snowball fight or fun thing, so I figured she could use a break like that after what she was dealing with. Besides some time spent out in the night air was a welcome change. The walk didn't take long to shovel even with all that had fallen. Since there was a lot of snow, it looked like there wouldn't be school the next day. The snow looked so thick and it was coming down so hard, there didn't seem to be an end in sight.

When it was like that, one of our favorite things to do was to pile in the Big Guy's truck and go four wheeling around town. We would drive through the slippery streets sliding around and laughing. The Big Guy would talk to his truck the whole time as if trying to tell it to turn or to slow down when it wouldn't do either. He always would find an empty parking lot to do dittos in. In case you don't know what, a ditto is, it's driving around in a small circle usually sliding more than anything. It can be dangerous as you could slide into something you didn't mean to. That's why he usually did it in the center of an empty parking lot. It sure is a lot of fun to do in the deep snow.

Since driving around with him like that was normally so much fun; we decided to go for a drive that night. We were out there driving around for a while before we realized how late it was. We had her laughing and having some fun and just lost track of time. To hear her laugh was good, so the whole thing was well worth it. We got back to the house a mite late, but we didn't worry about it. We pretty much figured school would get called off and we would be able to sleep in for a change. I think it was good for her as she smiled on her way home.

Of course, we had school the next day so we were all real tired and I got hollered at later because mom was mad, I left her alone with the parents. She always considered them weird and didn't like to talk to them much. I couldn't understand why it was so hard for her to talk with them for a while then excuse herself so she could go home after a bit. After all, I did tell her where I was going and what I was going to do. We only went driving to try to cheer up my friend. It was okay, like I said, I could do nothing right.

When things like this happen, sometimes it brings out the best in some folks and sometimes it brings out the worst. I don't know what it brought out in me. I didn't know much those first few days. I was in a haze. A much as I tried, I couldn't figure out why she did it. I knew she wasn't in her right mind to do such a thing because the girl I knew was very soft-hearted and wouldn't have hurt a fly.

Once, her father took a nuisance of a squirrel he trapped in the house out in the country and shot it because he was afraid if he let it lose it would just come back. It had chewed its way into their attic and created a pretty good mess. She was furious with her father for killing the poor thing and made him promise not to ever shoot any living creature again. That was the girl who turned the same gun on herself.

Every bone in my body screamed something was wrong. I carried so much guilt I can't tell you how bad it was. For years after wards, I couldn't even come to terms with what had happened. In my eyes, I had let her down when she cried out for help. I had seen it and identified it and chose to ignore it. I wanted so bad to be happy, I chose to let down a friend in need. That was something that was very hard to live with.

Since then and many years later, I've come to understand that even if I did try to make her tell me what was wrong that day, I probably couldn't have stopped what she did. After all, she knew me and she knew I would listen to her and try to help. It's what I've always done and she knew it. If she wanted my help, she would have asked for it and let me help. She made her decision on what to do without any regard for anyone else important in her life. I feel sorry she chose her path, but I know now I couldn't have stopped it. It took me many years to come to terms with this.

I had my thoughts on why she did what she did. Nothing that I could prove of course, but things that I remembered in the past added up now. I don't want to point fingers at anyone, but actions and events pointed to what she did and why she did it. I could see changes in her that I didn't like. Like I said, there really was nothing I could do, but it didn't stop me from feeling like maybe there was something I could have done or even should have done even before it got to that point.

As I said before, my friend was hefty. A few years back, her mom decided they would both try Weight Watchers. It worked for the most part for her. She lost a lot of weight and looked pretty good. She seemed pretty happy until it all stopped one day. I noticed she didn't look as clean as she used to and she started to gain some of that weight back. It wasn't long before she gained it all back and was just like she used to be only she didn't have that same sparkle she once had. Her laugh had changed and she didn't seem as carefree as she once was. I never asked and she never told. I will leave the story at that because she is gone. There is nothing I can do to bring her back.

Her sister was a different story. As I said, she was sicklier and more prone to being picked on. I always stood up for her where I could, but she also angered me. She always tried to be so much smarter than everyone which is one reason why she got picked on so bad. Every day, she had a new huge word that I had no clue what it meant. I always got the feeling she was speaking down to me like she thought I was stupid. That part was what angered me, but I would often let it go because after all, she was my friend. I put up with her weirdness for our friendship's sake. Things were strained between us after her sister died.

It was something we didn't like to talk about and the things we had in common seemed to disappear. Much later after I decided to marry the Big Guy, I know she wanted me to ask her to be one of my bridesmaids. At the time I was tired of her attitude and her weirdness and I really didn't want her in my wedding party. When I look back now, I wish I would have, but as I said before, I can't change the past or know the future.

It was years later, she had found a husband and moved away down to Arizona somewhere. I heard she got sick and came home to die. I wasn't sure what the sickness was, but when I got word, she was in the hospital, I went to see her. She was sick all right. She had a very fast-growing cancer. She was dying at a very young age of 27.

It turns out when they first found the cancer it

was the size of a grapefruit, and was in the midst of surgery when she had a stroke. Her husband insisted therapy for the stroke was more important than Kemo for fighting the return of the cancer. It came back alright. It was about the size of a basketball the second time and came back so fast. When I went to the hospital to see her, she was pretty much out of it. She recognized me, but was talking gibberish. I agreed with what she said even though I knew it was all wrong. I was very much saddened that day I left that hospital. A part of my child hood was dying with her. I could feel it.

It was a few weeks later when I was lying in bed early one morning. The Big Guy and I would listen to the radio to hear the obituaries before we got up to start our day. It was silly, but we'd say we had to listen to see if we had died in the middle of the night. If our names were called, then we knew we didn't have to get out of bed that day and we could just stay together. My name was almost called once. It was pretty close, but it wasn't quite right. I had to get up that day.

The day I heard her name I knew it was her even though the radio announcer mispronounced it. I called the radio station to correct it. I told the lady, my friend hated to have her name mispronounced and besides no one would know it was her if she didn't say it right. I remembered about her constantly complaining and being very angry when some would do that in school. When the radio person asked who I was, I just said I was an old friend of no importance and hung up.

Life sure changed. Friends were gone and time

flew by. I sometimes sit and wonder just where did that time go and ask why certain things happened the way they did. I didn't know why when it happened and I thought maybe somehow the answer would come to me. I still don't know the answer to either question. I'm not sure I ever will.

Chapter 8

Life changes so fast sometimes you can see it and sometimes you can't. The second it changed for me was at my friend's funeral. I didn't see it right off. Those first days after she died were horrible for me. I walked around in a daze. I was mean and ornery and I don't think I could see or think straight. I ran across those same girls that laughed and made fun of my friend before she shot herself. When they found out she really died, all they could do was laugh about it. I got so angry. I wanted to tear their heads off. I have never liked those girls since and wished nothing but heartache for them.

That first day back to school, when I didn't want to go, my mom's boyfriend gave me a ride. I told him I really didn't want to go. He told me something that day that I believe is one of the truest things I have ever heard. He said, "You know, there are only two things in this world that you will ever really have to do. Pay taxes and die." That was it. We were quiet the rest of the way to school that day.

As I sat down in my chair in band, I tried hard to keep my composure. So many memories were flying around and all I wanted to do was go home and cry. I was doing good until choir when the older sister walked in the music room carrying her sister's tuba. She was returning it to school. I took one look at it and I lost it. I had to leave the room.

One of my friends took me out and we went into the girl's locker room and I beat up the first locker I came to. I don't know if the gym teacher was in there because she never came out to see what the noise was or anything. I just sat there and cried. I wanted so bad to go home and curl up in a ball and never face the world again. But I couldn't do that. I had to keep going.

My friend walked me home and tried to console me. She didn't seem to be helping much, so she called the Big Guy to come over. He was there so fast; I hardly knew any time passed at all. I later found out he drove his truck like a mad man to get to me. When my friend said I needed him now, he knew I wasn't good. He took a short cut and drove right through the old cemetery behind my house. Even though it had cut off quite a few blocks, he could have damaged his truck if he hit a hidden gravestone. He said he didn't care about the truck; he just cared about getting to me as fast as he could. He later told me he plowed the snow so fast driving through it, it sprayed like a fountain.

Whenever I was with the Big Guy, I felt instantly better. My friend seemed to know this and was relieved to have him there. We talked for a while and spent some more time just being together. Mom later got mad about this because she was already starting to complain we were together too much. She just didn't understand how I needed him and how I was beginning to depend on him. It just got worse from there.

My friend's funeral was pretty sad. The family was huddled together and looked so small and sad. Broken maybe is a good word to describe how they became. My mom and the Big Guy went with me to the funeral and I sat in the middle between them. I didn't know it at the time, but my life was about to change again.

The second the priest said to give each other the offering of peace, I grabbed the Big Guy's hand and he reached over and kissed me on the lips right there in front of my mother. I shook my mom's hand and she kissed my cheek as well, but she had this strange look in her eye. I didn't understand what it would mean until that evening. I come to understand it was the start of all my troubles.

Later that night, after mom went to her bed, she called me in to talk to her. I was a little worried because it usually meant it was something serious. She told me she was forbidding me to see or to spend any more time with the Big Guy. She said she saw something today she didn't like and she thought it was best if I didn't see him anymore. I was dazed, again.

I could not believe at my age she was trying to tell me what to do. I was eighteen years old. I was almost graduated from high school. I was so close to being on my own, I could taste it and she was there dictating to me who I was to talk to and who I was not to talk to. When I asked her why she was doing this, she told me she would never tell me why and I was just to listen to her and do as she said to do. I was not to ask why. I told her I was disappointed.

Didn't she know me better than that? What kind of a person would I be if I go back on everything she taught? She told me to use my own brain and decide what I thought was right. Mom taught me not to let anyone tell me what to do, what was right and what was not. She taught me to always stand up for what I believed in.

It was one of those grandma sayings again, "Don't do as I do, do as I say." Personally, I never liked this one and vowed to never say or do that to any of my own children whenever I had them. I was going to lead by example and not by an iron thumb. I just could not understand how she expected me to listen to her when every bone in my body and when my heart screamed, "NO THIS IS NOT RIGHT!"

What I believed in; was you stand by a friend. The Big Guy had never been anything but a good friend. He was never mean and he had never hurt me. I was quite attached to him and if I stopped seeing him, I knew I would be miserable. I could not let her dictate who I should be friends with and who I should not be friends with. Especially since I had no good reason; and she could give me no good reason why he needed to be thrown away. I told her that night that I was not defying her to make her angry; I was defying her to keep me happy.

For that I paid dearly. She was so angry with me for a long time; it really made my life hell. I could no longer do anything at all right. I could every now and then before this time make her happy, but after that night, I don't think I ever did anything that pleased her ever again. My whole world changed again in one moment. I went from happy and carefree to upset and sad to confused and befuddled and in the doghouse in such a short time. It made my head spin to think of how fast it was.

My rules changed and her attitude towards me changed. Like I said, I could do no right. The more she yelled at me and forbid me to see the Big Guy, the more I snuck off to be with him. I just stopped caring what she wanted anymore. My time with the Big Guy was my forbidden fruit. I just couldn't understand why she felt that way. I could see no wrong in what I was doing, especially when I felt so good when I was with him. It just didn't make any sense to me. Now when I think back on it, mom was just trying to protect me the best she could but at the time, I couldn't see it.

I remember the first time the Big Guy kissed me. He kissed me several times since, well, okay, more than that, but there were a few first ones that really stood out. The very first kiss of friendship was during one night when we were playing music. He found out it was my 18th birthday and had a gift for me. It was a necklace and it was my birthstone. He said he wanted to give me a birthday kiss. He kissed me right on the lips. He smiled at me and said, "I want another!" He kissed me again after practice and the last was on my cheek before I went home. It was a gentle kiss. It surprised me because I didn't think anyone would ever want to kiss me like that. And I didn't think that big strong guy could be that gentle.

I remember the first real French kiss. He had brought me home after practice one night. I took him to my room because I wanted him to hear a song I liked and see if he wanted to learn to play it. While I played it on my stereo in my room, he stood in the doorway listening. He said he knew the song and it wouldn't be that hard to play and he was going to learn it for me.

After the song quit there was a little silence. The only noise there that was heard was a light rocking noise that came from the attic. He asked what that noise was. I told him not to worry; it was only Grandpa who looked out for me.

I believed there was a spirit in the house because I could hear it at times and had no other explanation of the noise it made or of different things that had happened. I got up to walk him out and right there in the middle of my doorway, he kissed me again. It was a kiss that made me light headed and dizzy. It felt so good and I really was not sure what to do next. It had happened so quick and lasted so long, I didn't know what to do about it.

After all, my mom was just there sitting in the living room. I didn't want to do anything improper. It was just the first of many kisses we would share. I'm not for sure on this, but I felt my grandpa was saying, "This guy is okay." I used to lie awake at night listening to the noise he was making in the attic. Now there really is no proof of what this was as no one could explain why the creaking noise came from that end of the attic.

This end had nothing but boxes stacked which made things harder to believe. In my heart, I knew what it was. Mom always called me crazy that no such thing existed, but I knew. I more felt it than anything. That night the noise was saying, "It's going to be alright."

Mom had heard bad things about the Big Guy and she was sure they were true. She didn't stop to ask him if they were or not, she just chose to believe them. That riled me, because if I heard something, I would ask him about the truth of the matter. From the way he looked me square in my eye and from the seriousness of his voice, I knew he wasn't lying. I couldn't see why she couldn't do the same. She just didn't know him like I did. She would warn me over and over that he was just after me because he found out I had a little money in the bank. She swore that when my money was gone, he would be gone.

I guess she didn't know what she thought she did, because even though that money didn't last at all, he never left. He promised me he would never leave no matter what and that is one promise he has always kept. Oh, every now and then, he will ask me if I have some of that money left and I always say, "Yep I do." He responds with, "Good, cause once it's gone, so am I!" There is usually a penny or some change in my pocket when I answer, so in a way, I'm not lying. But I know he is not leaving either. It is just a joke between us that we laugh about.

Mom just could not forgive me for not listening to her. She did everything she could to break us up. She changed my curfew from 11 pm to 10 pm on the weekends. She also grounded me from driving her car which I really didn't mind because the Big Guy started letting me drive his truck more and more. She started to complain about it and told me I was not to park that pile of junk in front of her house. I just started parking it up back behind the house. After she caught us together one night late and being up the rest of the night yelling at me, she decided if I was old enough to have relations, then I was old enough to paying $20.00 a week rent.

I know we shouldn't have spent the night together, but I wanted to be near him so bad. Mom was gone on one of her trips and not due back until sometime the next day, so I figured we were safe. I was wrong and she came home early and caught us. It was a really bad night and I knew I was in the wrong in one sense but right in another because I had never felt that way about any man in my life. I knew it was a love that would last, but she just saw it as me being a slut.

Remember how I told you she took her car away from me? Well, she didn't take my chores away and one day long after I quit driving her car, I decided to mow the grass. I went into the garage to get the riding mower and I could not believe my eyes. She had this round table stored in the garage and it sat ahead of where the car was always parked. I can remember her telling me every time I parked the car in the garage, to be careful of that dang table and whatever I did, I was not to hit it.

That day when I went to get the mower out, I noticed that dang table. In the side was a huge hole the same size as her right light on her car. I knew I didn't do it because I hadn't driven her car in months. Not since way last winter. I had to ask her what happened to that table. She wouldn't talk much about it. All she'd say is the car slid on some ice and banged into it.

Personally, I think one of those many nights she was mad at me, she whipped into the garage and hit the table. Again, I have no proof. I can only laugh about it now. Years later, she gave me the table which the Big Guy promptly fixed and repainted. I still have it as a memory and to this day I won't give it up.

I still got into a lot of trouble by being late many nights. I would go where I wanted to, but I knew I had to be home on time. When it got close to being time to go, I would tell the Big Guy, "I have to go home." He'd say, "Well, give me a kiss goodbye." and we'd start kissing. We'd be standing in his mom's hallway just holding each other and kissing.

When we would break, that's when I'd be in trouble because I'd look at the clock and without us knowing, an hour had passed. Since I only had ten minutes when we started kissing, I knew I was way late and in trouble, again. He'd walk me home in the snow and we'd just hold each other to keep warm. It always felt bad to know he had to walk back alone, but he didn't seem to mind. I would be in more trouble because we'd kiss again at my house. I was in trouble a lot.

Some of my troubles were in school too. I wasn't a bad kid by any means. I just wasn't a favorite of some teachers. Until I was a senior I pretty much walked on the line and let a lot of things slide. I didn't stand up for myself much and I pretty much took the crap people gave me. After spending all that time with the Big Guy, he started to teach me to stand up for myself. I remember one teacher in particular who really didn't like me at all. I don't think she liked the Big Guy any better, because she even took me aside once and told me I shouldn't be dating him. I couldn't believe her nerve and I told her flat out it was none of her business and walked away from her. I think that is when she really started to be out to get me.

She was my publications teacher and I needed the credit to graduate. We were the class who made up the yearbook. Everyone in the class had to walk around taking pictures of everyone and then we'd make up pages for the yearbook. I remember working hard on my assigned pages. I spent hours getting them just right. After I handed them in, the teacher didn't seem to look at them at all, she just set them on her desk and told me to go read something.

The next day, I noticed one of her "pets" was working on a page. I knew that most of the pages were almost done, so I wondered what she was doing. As I got closer, I recognized the work I had already done. Here, the teacher had handed my page to her and told her to redo it. I was so angry. After that in her class I either was out taking pictures, or sitting there reading a newspaper or working on my homework for another class. Once, she told me I should work on things for her class, I asked her "Why so you could have your pet to redo my work?" She just walked away mad.

She was also the teacher I had to deal with in my study hall after lunch. I never liked her and was always quiet and did my work. Every now and then because I would lose track of time being with the Big Guy at lunch, I would come in to study hall a few minutes late. Back then, if you were 18, you could write your own notes to make it an excused tardy. So, when I was late, I would write myself a note, take it to the office and it would be excused. Things worked out pretty good until one day.

On one of our many travels when we were

spending time together, we ran across an ad for free German Sheppard puppies. Since I loved animals the Big Guy and I went to look at them. It was rare that anyone would be giving away purebred Sheppard's for free. When we got there, we met with the people. They had to move and couldn't take the dogs with them, so they had to find them homes quick or put them to sleep.

After seeing all those cute pups, there was no way we could imagine them killing them, so the Big Guy said we'd take one. We picked out a female pup and was she ever cute. We didn't get papers on her, but we didn't care. I had always wanted my own dog. That was something I was never allowed at home. The most I could ever have was a cat outside. The Big Guy smiled at me and said, "Happy Graduation! She is yours!" I was so excited, but worried at the same time. I knew mom would never let me keep a dog at home. Even after she seen the pup, I was right. There was no way that pup was staying at my house.

The Big Guy loved dogs too so he snuck the pup into his apartment for as long as he could. It lasted about three weeks before he was caught because of the noise and was told to get rid of the pup. We tried to find anyone we could to help us take care of her, but no one wanted to help. We took the pup home to the Big Guy's mom and asked her as a last resort.

We explained that we would get her back as soon as we were married and had our own place. His mom fell instantly in love with that pup and said she'd take care of her. His dad growled and said, "There is not going to be no dam dog in my house!" She told him right quick that, "This was MY house and if I want this pup there, then it would be here!" He didn't say any more about it and she was our pup sitter for the time being.

It was shortly after the Big Guy's mom agreed to keep the pup. I still continued to go to her house for lunch. We were out spending a few minutes with the pup when I realized I had to get back to school. The Big Guy had to take his mom to the doctor's office so we all left really quickly. After I got to school, I had this sinking feeling I had forgotten to put a rope on the pup.

I knew we had left her loose in the back yard. It would be hours before someone would be back on the house to check on her. I knew she would wander off or get hurt, so I walked in the office at school and told them about my problem. I said, "I'd call, but no one is home there. Is it okay, if I drive back, tie the pup and get right back?" They told me it was fine. All I had to do was write myself a note and it would be an excused lateness. So, I did what they told me to do.

When I got back to school, I walked into this teacher's class and handed her the note from the office that excused my tardiness. She read it, tore it up and said, "This don't work for me. You have a detention tonight!" She told me to meet her up in the study hall after school. I tried to tell her I had a job I had to get to, but she didn't care.

Between classes I called the Big Guy and told him what happened. I didn't want him to be waiting around after school for me and I asked him to call my work to tell them I'd be late. Well, the Big Guy was there after school anyway. He was talking to his good friend who was a janitor at the school. Mom had called the school earlier and told the principle she didn't want him on school grounds to get me. Like I told you, she did everything she could to break us up.

As the Big Guy walked through the hall with his friend, he was being told, "You know you shouldn't be here." He said, he was here to pick me up and there was nothing anyone could do about it. He must have looked pretty angry about the whole thing because even though the principal seen him in the hall, sat back down and pretended to work like he hadn't seen him there. No one did anything to ask him to leave.

I was waiting up at the study hall when this teacher from hell and the janitor walked in. I wanted to get the detention over as quick as I could so I could get back to work and not be in too much trouble there. The teacher told the janitor to have me wash desks for my punishment. He said he would and she walked out.

He looked at me and smiled. I said, "Well, what do you want me to do?" He says, "See this can of spray?" I go, "Yea." He says, "Spray that desktop." So, I did. He says, "See this rag?" he held up? I say, "Yea." He says, "Take it and wipe that desktop off." I did. He takes both the can and the rag from my hands and smiles again. He says, "Good, now get the hell out of here, you cleaned a desk. Be sure you go out the back way!" I smiled and said "You got it! Thanks!" I left as quick as I could, laughing all the way. I made it to work and I wasn't even late. It's good to have friends in low places!

The Big Guy had already asked me three times to marry him and for the first few, I always said no. The very first time he asked, he even laughed it off as a joke, but deep down, I knew he was serious. He had asked me to walk on his back and crack it for him. After I did, he got up and asked said, "Will you marry me?" As he laughed about it, I saw a look in his eyes that said he was serious. I didn't think I was ready for that, so I laughed it off as well.

The next time he asked, it was deer season and I was out riding with him. He pulled up by the local pond and we just sat there holding each other when he asked me again. I said, "Yes" this time and everything seemed to change again. I was still confused, but I wanted to be happy with him.

Back then I guess I didn't weight all that much. During our Kempo lessons, some of the guys complained about the push-ups the instructor asked them to do. He wanted them to practice knuckle push-ups to increase their strength. The Big Guy got tired of hearing their whining and without saying anything he got down by a wall and got his feet up on the wall and started to do push-ups.

This got their attention right quick. After he did 50 or so, he jumps up and tells me to come over to him. He gets down like he is going to do more pushups and tells me to sit on his shoulders. I do and he starts to do knuckle push-ups with me sitting right there. I was pretty amazed and without telling me, he switches and only uses one hand. The guys about dropped their jaws and quit complaining right quick. They saw the strength and really didn't want to irritate him anymore. It sure got my attention too!

One of the last times I was with my old boyfriend was shortly after I said yes for the third time to the Big Guy. I was still so confused and I was hearing so many different stories. I didn't think I had any feelings for my old boyfriend, but I had to be sure. I went one last night to decide what I was really doing. When he asked me if I wanted to fool around, I tried to see what it felt like. It was no way as good, or comfortable or safe as it was with the Big Guy so I stopped it just after things started to happen. I told him I was sorry, but I didn't love him and it wasn't right to be doing such things. I was actually here to tell him goodbye and not to contact me again.

He seemed very disappointed and tried to talk me out of it. I argued with him for a while and gave up and just left to go be with the Big Guy. He is the one I wanted to be with. I later found out the Big Guy seen me with him that last night and was very confused and upset and hurt by it. I always skirted the subject because I was ashamed, I had to even resort to that to straighten out my head. The Big Guy was hurt for a long time over it because he thought he had lost me.

Long after we were together and I could finally talk about it, I told him the truth. He seemed angry still until I told him he just didn't understand. That was not the night he almost lost me, that was the night he truly gained me. I could finally see and feel what was right. It was like a huge cloud of doubt was raised off my mind and I could really see who it was that loved and cared about me unconditionally.

It seemed like no matter what happened, the bad times always brought the Big Guy and me closer together. Things that were meant to pull us apart, just worked the opposite. We have been through so much and survived a lot of heartache and pain; I believe we can survive most anything. For as much as we have suffered together, we have had good times too. So many good memories of being together, of laughing and joking are around. We raised our kids and did the best we could. We started traditions where there were none before. All in all, I can tell you what we lived through was well worth it. Is that not what life is after all?

I remember one night everything almost stopped. I went down to my Kempo class one night to find the Big Guy. I was very upset. My mom had been on me because she was mad about me spending time with the Big Guy during my class. I knew she was right, but with all the badgering she gave me, I agreed that I wouldn't let him be there anymore when I was taking my lesson.

I know, it was dumb, but I was under a lot of stress and I really wanted mom to back off. As I walked in through the door, I saw him. I knew he was waiting for me. I tried to tell him as gentle as I could that when I was down here, he couldn't be anymore. He got mad at me because he thought if I gave in to my mom on this, I would give in to her about breaking up with him. That is not what I meant at all. I was trying to please both parties to try to make my life more bearable at home.

He got very angry and walked out. I stayed there only for a few minutes before I left. Since I didn't feel like working out, I decided to go home and maybe shut myself in my room so I could sleep. As I walked down the street, I saw him punch the pop machine down by the old grocery store. I was heartbroken because I thought he was going to start drinking and he probably would be drinking a lot, he was that mad. I didn't want to deal with that, so I turned the corner towards home.

I didn't make it very far before he caught up with me. He told me he was sorry and we'd work it out no matter what happened. He held me while I cried again. I told him I was sorry and I didn't want to break up with him. I had his ring and I wasn't about to give it up. Ah, the ring, that is another memory.

That next class night, I was down at the shop without the Big Guy like I promised. I was well into my lesson when he came through the door. I was starting to ask him what he was doing down here because he wasn't supposed to be here. He said he knew that but he had a story that I would be very interested in. He said he was walking out his door when he noticed my mom's car sitting in the parking lot across from his house. He was only going to get something he needed out of his truck.

My mom realized she was seen, so she took off wildly down the street to try to get away. The roads were a little slippery and she slid into the snow bank and got stuck. The Big Guy thought it was funny she got caught spying on him when he was doing nothing wrong. He got in his truck and drove down to her and offered to help her get out of the bank. He said, "Do you want a tow?" She said, "Just leave me alone!" She was heated up, so the Big Guy said, "Okay." and drove off. He came down to tell me about it. I guess she spun her tires until she got herself out. We both got a good laugh about it and she never said one word about what happened.

I think maybe this was the night she ran into that

table in her garage, but I don't know for sure. She would never admit it to me and all I have is my speculation, a laugh and the table.

It was Valentine's Day and I had to be at school. I didn't seem to want to be there anymore. I was so tired of the teachers and the other kids. The way they acted and the way they treated me was just getting on my nerves. I didn't care anymore about being there. I still did my work, but I counted the hours and minutes before I could leave again and be with him.

I was in class and looking at the clock just counting the minutes before the bell would ring and I could go to lunch. The Big Guy took to meeting me for lunch so we could spend some more time together. I cherished every second we stole. I hated it when I had to leave him and loved it when we were together.

The bell finally rang and I headed for my locker and then to find the Big Guy. Well, what can I say? The Big Guy found me first. I was in the hall right by the school trophy case. I saw him and hurried towards him. I wanted to give him a quick kiss so no one would see, but as he got to me, he grabbed my hand and went down on one knee. He handed me an open box and asked, "Will you marry me??" My jaw dropped open; I was so amazed. He did this at the most opportune time too. Not only was I standing there, but I was standing there surrounded by many so called "friends".

A couple of years before, these same friends had gotten mad at me. I remember I had talked to a boy who was in my math class. The kid was a new kid, he was from Hawaii and one of my best friends had a crush on him. His locker was near mine and one day, started talking to me about class stuff. My friend saw it and got mad because she thought I was "hitting" on her "boyfriend".

Number one, he wasn't her boyfriend, he didn't even like her and number two, like I said before, no one tells me who I talk to and who I don't talk to. I got mad right back and it started this huge fight. To be mean, they all told me I was not good enough to ever get a boyfriend. I had to resort to stealing theirs. If I did find some boy stupid enough to date me, I wouldn't know what to do with him anyway! They were very mean and vicious. This fight went on for almost half a school year and it really left me with a bad taste in my mouth. After that when we supposedly made up and were friends again, I never felt the same or trusted them as I did before ever again.

When the Big Guy asked me to marry him on bent knee and with an engagement ring to boot right in front of them, I almost died. They screamed and ogled at the ring. They all hugged me and told me how lucky I and how great it was. Of course, he took the ring and put it on my finger and I kissed him in front of everyone.

It was a wonderful day! I was so excited! I knew I couldn't show my mom right away, because she'd go through the roof, but it was the fact that he had worked and bought a ring just for me that made me so happy. I knew he worked hard for it. He didn't have much money and when he bought something, it meant he busted his backside to earn the cash he needed. No one gave him anything.

I later found out he worked and saved for months to be able to pay for that ring. He told me it wasn't exactly the ring he wanted for me, but it was the one he could afford. He promised me one day, he would buy me a better ring with a bigger diamond. I told him I didn't care what size stone the ring had. That ring meant the world to me because it represented our love. I didn't care if it came from a bubble gum machine or a Cracker Jack box!

Yes, it had been quite an interesting couple of months. I was so tired. I was tired of bad things happening. I was tired of fighting with my mom. But most of all, I was tired of hiding my love for my man. He was not the perfect man in the eyes of a lot of folks in town, but for me he was the love of my life. If people would just leave us alone and let us live as we let them live, we would be fine. If they didn't, that was okay too because as long as we were together, we knew our love would survive anything. And it did.

Chapter 9

I remember how pretty that Valentine's Day was. It should have been elbow deep with snow and blowing cold. But it wasn't. The sun was out, there were huge spots where the grass showed and I was outside wearing a T-shirt. The Big Guy had gotten me my ring and I was so happy. He had also gotten me a big bouquet of flowers. He got the same for his mom and we were heading over to her house to give it to her. She seemed to be very happy for us when I showed her my ring.

The Big Guy's dad however was different. Since I was not used to many men, he scared me. I never felt comfortable around him, so when I was, I was very polite and quiet. I felt the same about his brother as he was a big man too. Back then I was very shy and quiet and it didn't take much to make me afraid.

I remember what his brother said about me after the Big Guy first brought me home to meet his family. He asked his brother what he thought of me. I was so worried what they thought, I could hardly stand it. His brother thought I was nice and said, "But she's a bit short, isn't she?" I about died when he told me that. Of all things he could say, he commented on my height. I think you all know what I would be battling for the next upcoming years!

I couldn't believe his dad laughed at us when I showed him my ring. The Big Guy's mom scolded her husband for laughing, but I smiled and walked away just the same. The Big Guy told me not to worry about it; that his dad liked me just fine. I tried not to worry about it too much because I already had to worry about showing my mother the ring.

We went to mom's house with some flowers for her and showed her the ring. She was not happy. She had that pissed off look like she always had whenever I did something she didn't like. I knew I was in for it, but I was getting to the point where I didn't care. Mom continually got argumentative. She found fault with everything I did even more so from then on. I only had a few months of school left and I was very close to moving out of the house anyway so I decided to try to live with it and fight less.

She would lose her temper with me a lot and tell me to just get it over and move out. She'd scream at me, "GET OUT!" I'd always leave and go spend time with the Big Guy because he always made me feel better. I told him I didn't know how much more I could take. She kept telling me to get out and since I couldn't stand the way she was treating me, I wanted to get out. The Big Guy told me I didn't have to take that. He told me to pack my stuff and he'd find me a place to stay.

I couldn't move in with him and his parents. That wasn't something I would have even asked. There is no way I would have ever done that. He told me not to worry; he had a friend who had a room I could stay in. So, he gave me one of his army bags and I went home and started to slowly put my clothes and things in the bag. I kept the bag in my closet so mom couldn't see what I was doing. I really didn't want the fight it would cause if she saw it. Besides that, I wanted to be ready for the next time she told me to get out. Then instead of arguing with her, I'd just say, "Fine, I'm out of here!" It was pretty quiet for the next few days, so I just continued to put stuff in the bag quietly.

One night as I was heading out the door, she called me back. I went to her out of respect and because she didn't say it mean. She asked if she could talk to me and I said yes, she could always talk to me. She says, "So, your planning another little surprise for me?" I asked her what she meant. She told me she found my packed bag in the closet. She wanted to know when I had planned on leaving. I knew what that meant. It meant she had been looking through my things. I wondered how long she had been doing that.

I told her I didn't want to leave, but I had no choice as I couldn't take her telling me to get out anymore. She started crying and said she didn't want me to leave. She admitted the only reason why she said that was because she wanted to find a way to control me and make me do what she wanted. I suppose in her mind, I wouldn't have anywhere else to go and I would have to start listening and do what she wanted. I told her I was an adult now making my own decisions.

I was trying to do the best I could but I couldn't take her yelling at me for every little thing. If she wanted me to stay, I would, but I would not take that abuse. She said she was sorry and she would try. I hugged her and told her I loved her, but I had to go because I was late. I believe I had to go to school for pep band to play at a game. I knew the teacher would be mad, but I was one who always showed for her no matter what. I knew she wouldn't be mad at me for long. Things got a little better after that. Not much, but a little.

The next few months were a blur. I kept up with my studies and got straight A's. I thought my mom would finally be proud of me, but she never showed it. I was really disappointed. My whole school career, all I wanted to do was get good grades to have her proud of me.

My older sister lived in the National Honor Society with every report card. I wanted to be like her, but I could never seem to do what she did to get there. I know she had her ways. I won't say what she did and give youngsters bad ideas. And I don't want to be judging what she did, but in my book, it was wrong. I can't say she cheated every time, but I know she did a lot of times.

I always was taught to be honest. A person's trust was pretty easy to get the first time, but if you do something and lose someone's trust, it takes a long time and is dang near impossible to earn back. There is always a shadow of doubt and I sure didn't want any shadows hanging around me. Oh, I had my close calls and pushed the limits, but found out it was not worth it.

I remember once in middle school; I answered some questions pretty quickly and did them really sloppy. I was feeling bad about how bad it looked. I of course, got the answers wrong anyway. I know I shouldn't have, but I erased the answers, rewrote them neater and then marked them wrong as we were checking them with the whole class.

I know there was someone who saw me and told on me because the teacher talked to me about it. She wanted to know why I was cheating. I told her I wasn't, just trying to make my paper neater like I should have done in the first place. I told her I marked the answers wrong when we corrected it, but I didn't want it to be so sloppy. She told me next time not to worry about the sloppiness of it, just as long as I wasn't cheating.

I was beginning to not care what people thought of me. There was a time when I used to care big time. I went through that stage where as a young girl you think you need make up. I'm sure all you ladies have been in that stage or maybe never even got out of it. It's where you're asked to go somewhere on the spur of the moment and all you can think of is "I need to put my face on," before you can go. As I said before, I had terrible acne and I thought the makeup helped to hide it. Of course, it didn't and most times, it just made it worse. Now, I was at a stage where I didn't care what I looked like.

I dressed for comfort. I wore my hair the way I liked it. I hardly ever put on makeup. I know at times I might have looked like a slob, but I didn't care. When I had to dress up for something special, that's when I went all out. I'd curl my hair, wore makeup and put on nice jewelry. I'd try to dress nice for what I had. I know I never wore designer clothes, but that was because I could never afford them. I bought my clothes on sale from places like K-mart. I bought what I liked, not what was in style. I might have not been the best dressed, but when I did dress up, I didn't think I looked too bad.

I remember getting ready for a Christmas party for work one year. I had decided to go all out and look really nice for it. I asked the Big Guy if he wanted to go with. It was being held at a pretty nice place, so I knew I wouldn't be out of line in dressing up. The Big Guy thought it was a great idea. I wore my new red dress the Big Guy bought for me after having our first child. I went all out. I curled my hair, wore makeup and got jewelry to match the dress. I looked pretty good if I do say so myself.

Normally I wore jeans, t-shirts, flannel shirts and sweat shirts to work. No one had ever seen me dress up. That night I even felt pretty as we walked into the supper club. The Big Guy excused himself to get us a couple of drinks and while I was standing by myself when one of the guys, I worked with every day came up and stood by me. He hardly said hi and only nodded his head at me.

I looked at him for a while then asked, "Are you stuck up now or what? Aren't you going to talk to me at all?" I guess he hadn't said anything because he didn't even recognize me! He looked dumb founded when he realized who I was. He quickly apologized and said he thought I was someone's girlfriend and didn't want to get into trouble for talking to me. I laughed and told him it didn't matter because I would talk to him no matter where we were.

That was one thing the Big Guy loved about me. I didn't pretend to be something I was not. He said I was not fake like a lot of girls were. He really didn't like it when girls wore a lot of "war paint" as he called it. He said he loved the natural look and I was it for him.

I never considered my body to be the best. As I said before, I always seemed to be heavier than the rest of the girls in my class. Oh, there were a couple who were fatter, but the majority was pretty skinny and I was between 10-20 pounds heavier than them. This bothered me a lot and I seemed to always be on a diet. Not that I actually ate healthy, it was more like not eating at all. As much as I tried not to eat, I couldn't seem to lose anything. I'd have to be sick before I felt like I lost anything, then it would come back anyway.

Mom was always telling me to watch my weight. She was always warning me to be careful of what I ate or else I'd get fatter and fatter. I was never very tall, well okay, most folks would call me short, so weight would always seem to be more noticeable on me.

One thing the Big Guy was always telling me was he loved my body. He kept telling me it was perfect. I kept calling myself ugly and fat and he kept getting mad about it and telling me not to say that. I remember when we first became intimate; I was always so embarrassed over my body. I could only relax with him if the light was off. I would not want him to even look at me. He would laugh at how shy I was and couldn't understand why I felt that way or why I would say bad things about myself.

I couldn't help it. I spent so much time saying it, changing now was so difficult. It was also hard to believe him as it was totally opposite from what everyone else in the world had been telling me. He just kept telling me the others were jealous they didn't look like me and it was their loss. I don't know, maybe it was, maybe it wasn't. All I know is I had to learn how to deal with him giving me compliments like that. He always put me up on a pedestal. I just hoped I would never fall off.

The rest of the school year drudged on. I spent as much time with the Big Guy as I could, stayed in trouble with my mom and counted the days until I would graduate. The rest of the time, we had a wedding to plan. There was no way I was going to ask my mom to pay for it not only because I knew she wouldn't because she didn't like the Big Guy. I felt she couldn't afford it and I didn't want her to have to pay for it. Besides, I would never hear the end of it if she did pay. I just didn't want her to be able to throw that in my face. The Big Guy knew this and he agreed with me. We had long talks about what we both wanted and we started making lists of who we wanted in the wedding and what we wanted.

We were running into a major block. We couldn't get a priest to talk to us about planning the wedding. Every time we contacted one, we were told, he had no time to talk about it now to call back later. It got to the point where we realized my mom had already gotten to all the priests and told them all she didn't want us married. It was very aggravating.

I knew something had to be done about it, but more important, the Big Guy knew he had to do something about it. He even considered going to a different church to get married. This meant changing religions. He knew I wanted to get married in the

Catholic Church, so that would be one of our last resorts. I didn't know what to do.

Mom wanted us to wait until after I got out of college, I know she did. I didn't care, the only thing I knew is I loved the Big Guy and I wanted to spend the rest of my life with him. The Big Guy didn't want to wait either. He told me not to worry about it. He said he'd take care of everything. I believed him. I trusted him. He took care of everything. Maybe not in the absolute right way, but it got taken care of.

I was pretty naive when it came to a lot of things. I knew how things worked, but I guess I was pretty gullible. I didn't think premarital sex was right, but I loved the Big Guy so much. I knew it was wrong in the Church's eyes, but when you're looking at it through love's eyes, it's not wrong. I wanted to be careful as I didn't want to become pregnant. I stressed this to the Big Guy every day. I knew if I became pregnant, I would be done for in my mom's eyes.

I didn't want that to deal with on top of everything else. I know my mom was afraid I wouldn't go to college but I was determined. I knew the Big Guy wasn't thrilled with me going way for some reason, but I know he understood why I needed to go. I still tried to stick to my plan as much as I could.

I trusted the Big Guy more than I ever trusted anyone ever in my life. Some say I shouldn't have, but I did. I don't regret anything that happened. I know I wasn't ready for what happened next. I wasn't grown up enough or maybe I didn't want to be grown up yet.

I was late. I'm not talking late for an appointment. I missed my period. I prayed hard not to be pregnant. I worried about it constantly. I worried so much I made myself sick. I ended up with a high fever. I didn't want it to be true but I knew it was.

I was devastated. Everything I had planned for was ruined. The Big Guy didn't feel the same way. He told me he loved me and would stand by me no matter what. He told me if I didn't want him or the baby anymore, he'd take the baby and raise him or her by himself. I still wanted him; I just didn't know what to do.

Every time mom looked at me, I knew she knew only she wasn't saying. She finally commented on my weight one day and I really knew she knew. When we finally told her, she went through the roof. All I heard was how I ruined my life and why did I do this to her. Last time I checked it wasn't her that was pregnant. It was me.

I knew I wasn't ready for such a big step. The Big Guy was still prepared to marry me and stand by me and the baby. I wasn't sure I was ready to be a wife and a mother. I was just getting used to being a girlfriend. I had so much thinking to do. I was so afraid I wouldn't be a good mom. Already, I knew the Big Guy would make a great dad. It was me who I doubted. I had so many problems of my own I didn't want to compound them by mixing in a new life. I was so confused and disappointed in myself. Somehow, I knew I let everyone down. I felt I messed up big time.

I didn't know much, but I did know things were changing again. After graduation, planning for our wedding stepped up big time. The priest even started to talk to us. We told him I was pregnant and we had to get married. We gave him an ultimatum. If he didn't agree to marry us, tomorrow we would be Lutheran.

He agreed to marry us and we started going through the classes the priest wanted us to do. The Big Guy and I planned everything. We decided what we wanted and we scoured the area to find what we wanted as cheap as we could. We knew we had to pay for everything on our own. We would have no help to do what we wanted.

I've been wrong about certain people in my lifetime, but I've never been more wrong about his sister. In school I was friends with the Big Guy's little sister. I thought she was a good friend. She was quiet, sweet and funny. I really liked her a lot. I never heard her say one cross word to anyone. What the Big Guy told me about her was completely different. He told me about how nasty and ornery she was. How her mood swings were so terrible.

She even got him thrown out of the house once. He was sitting at the table trying to do some figuring for a job. She came up to him teasing him and really disturbing his concentration. He asked her several times to stop because he needed to think about what he was doing. Well, things went bad from there. She clawed his arm with her nails, and he hit her when he put his hand up. He didn't mean to hit her, it just happened because she was so close to him. Besides, it wasn't a hard hit, he was just trying to make her let loose of his arm. She hollered and his dad threw him out for "hitting" his sister.

The Big Guy was angry and left. Since he didn't have anywhere else to go, he took his tent and put it up in the woods where he hunted and that is where he stayed. It was winter time and his mom worried something fierce about him. He would come home only when his dad wasn't there and his mom would beg him to move back home. He reassured his mom that he was doing fine and he wasn't coming home. It was a lot of trouble started by his "angel" sister.

I would not believe him and I stuck up for her constantly. There is no way that sweet girl was like that, ever. Boy was I wrong. I apologize to him even to this day. She was nice at first. The closer it got to my wedding, the worse she got. All we heard from her and everyone is what we should do and how we should be handling our wedding.

Anything we said we wanted to do, we were told it was stupid and we shouldn't do it that way. It got very aggravating. Years after we were married, I distanced myself from her and only put up with her for the Big Guy's sake. Believe me, I was so wrong about her and it was more evident every day.

The Big Guy came really close to hitting her after we were married. She was mad at him for some reason and had started to dislike me. He was at his mom's having coffee one morning and she was angry because he was there. She asked him when was he going to stop mooching off of her mom and asked where was I and how did he know for sure the baby I was carrying was his.

Well, let me tell you, the Big Guy has never hit a woman. He came close to it that day! He told her to mind her own business because the coffee was his he was drinking. It was left over from our wedding. He said I was working and if she ever said anything bad like that again about me, she'd be in need of new teeth. Even his mom was upset. She had liked me and didn't like what her daughter was implying.

There was no way my baby was not the Big Guy's. We had spent so much time together; I just didn't have time to be with someone else. Besides the fact that I didn't want anyone else. I'm not sure why she said those horrible words that day. Maybe it was jealousy, maybe it was anger or just maybe she got up on the wrong side of the bed. It was the first time in many that I began to know how she truly was.

I was wrong about many things. I have learned from my mistakes. I guess that is why we are supposed to make them. As I told you, the priest started talking to us about our marriage. We were happy about that. It was finally coming true. We were finally going to be together. One night during one of our talks, the Big Guy came clean with me. I was feeling so down about being pregnant and being so hard on myself for being weak, he couldn't stand it anymore.

He told me it was his fault, not mine. Well, it was mine as well because it took two to tango, but that was beside the point he was making. I trusted him when he told me he was being safe and I wouldn't get pregnant. He lied. Apparently, he did that on purpose. He confessed he was very afraid of losing me and of not being able to marry me. He was afraid of the odds that were against him. With the priest refusing to marry us, with me wanting to go off to school and my mom not liking him, he was just afraid.

One thing he did know. He figured that if I was

pregnant, the priest would have to marry us. He knew if I was pregnant, I wouldn't go off to school so quick. With me carrying his child, my mom would eventually have to accept him as father of her grand baby. He knew a lot I didn't think of.

It might have been the wrong thing to do, but it was meant with the best intentions. I was upset with him. He should have talked to me about what he was doing because when he decided to do something that affected me more than him, that said he didn't care how I felt about it.

The path was already chosen. I was already walking down it. I could not go back. It didn't matter now what I wanted. I had a new person growing in me that I had to worry about.

Chapter 10

Graduation was finally here. It seemed so strange after all that time of wishing, dreaming and planning that the day had finally come. I was supposed to be grown up and the problem was, I didn't feel one bit different than I had when I was 17, 16, 15, 14 or even 13 for that matter. I had the same brain, same thoughts and same feelings. The thing that really scared me is I was supposed to be this mature woman and I was afraid I wasn't. I was starting to be more confused. When was this big change supposed to happen? I had no clue. What I was really afraid was what would I do if it never came to be?

High school was finally over for me. My last day of class was very happy because I kept thinking, tomorrow, I won't have to be here anymore! I remember thinking about all the bull crap things I wouldn't have to put up with anymore and it made me feel so relieved. I tried to think of all the things I would miss and frankly there were not too many. I had a few friends, but no one I would really call a true friend. Most of the kids in my class couldn't stand me and I couldn't stand them, so that was really no loss. Far as I could tell, the only thing I would probably regret was leaving home and not living with my mother anymore.

Come to think of it, after all the fights and arguments, that really wasn't such a bad thing after all. Don't get me wrong, I really loved my mother which is why I put up with a lot of crap from her. I really wanted to try to please her and kept trying to change her opinion on the Big Guy. I couldn't do either, but I continually tried. No, graduation day for me was a complete relief. As I look back on the pictures from that day, I see things I hadn't noticed back then.

For one, in all my pictures, I look like I'm about to cry. I think I probably was, but it's not what everyone thought. It was for tears of happiness that all my suffering was about to end. Most people thought I was sad my high school days were over, but it was the complete opposite. I was so happy; I couldn't hardly contain myself. I guess in times of emotional stress I cry. Not sure why, but it's what I do.

Another thing I noticed was how angry mom looked in all the pictures. There was not one taken of her with an honest smile on her face. I pretty much know why. I think to her it meant the time was soon coming when I'd be leaving and be living my own life without her at the helm.

Of course, the past months she wasn't controlling me like she wanted and I think it was the realization that she truly did not have any power over me was really coming into light for her. I had so wanted her proud of me, but now that I look back, pride was the furthest thing from her mind. She hated what I was doing, she hated who I was with and she thought I was throwing my life away with both hands.

I remember the ceremony plain as day. Some of my classmates were crying, some were laughing and some were constantly wishing others well. In my heart I just kept looking at them and knowing that the end of their so-called rein of power in high school would be over. I knew that in whatever school they would be deciding to go to, they would be the new kid, the freshy, the underdog and it made me smile.

I knew I would be in the same boat, but it was nice to know they would be brought down to my level for once. I just wanted the ceremony to be over and be done with it. It couldn't happen fast enough in my book.

My graduation party went pretty well. There were a lot of people who came to wish me well. I did confuse a few people however. See, remember I told you of who my sister's blood parents and grandparents were? I pretty much invited the same people my sister did when she graduated.

She introduced mom's brother and his wife as Grandma and Grandpa. I introduced them as Aunt and Uncle. I remember chuckling at all the strange looks and whispers I got. I thought to myself, good, let them try to figure that one out! If they went a little crazy trying it and didn't have the nerve to come out and ask, let them stew because I didn't care anymore what anyone thought.

The Big Guy was there for me and was proud as punch even if my mother was not. He attended the ceremony and was the first to get to me to congratulate me with a kiss. He knew how important it was for me to have him there because I was really feeling like my mother had already labeled me as an outcast. It made me happy to know at least one person was proud of my accomplishments.

I felt bad for him because he knew what rejection felt like. His own dad never even took the time to go to his graduation. This really saddened me because I knew how much it hurt him. I didn't know him then like I did now and I know if we did date back then, I'd have been the first to give him a kiss and congratulate him like he did for me.

I had worked hard and gotten an award. I felt bad because I didn't get one scholarship like I had hoped, and the award didn't have any monetary value. I earned the Louis Armstrong Jazz award. I was still proud of it no matter what because it was pretty hard to get. I know it didn't mean a thing to my mom because there was no dollar sign attached to it, but I was proud just the same. The trophy still sits on my book case today.

The Big Guy had gotten me flowers and bought me a boom box for my graduation present. The pup he gave me was the most important present even though my mom wouldn't let me keep her. I didn't care because it was a bundle of love given out of an even bigger love. She meant the world to me and mom just couldn't seem to understand why it was so important to me. I didn't care if she didn't understand because I was tired of trying to make her know why I did what I did. I could see the big picture even if she couldn't.

I got right to work on the arrangements for going on to school. I was going to prove to mom that no matter what I was completing my education and I would make something of myself. The day I got the letter from the school, I had applied to had crushed my spirits sadly. It was the letter you get when they are full up and they let you know you're on a waiting list.

The course I wanted only accepted 40 people out of the whole state and I was number three on their waiting list. I was devastated! The Big Guy held me while I cried and couldn't seem to understand why I was so hurt. He kept saying, you got number 3, that's really good.

I tried to explain it to him. It was because I always down on the list for everything my whole life. For once I wanted to make it. I wanted to be on the in list. Waiting was something I didn't want to do any more to fulfill my dreams. I think he understood, but he seemed relieved for some strange reason. It was beyond me to understand why he wasn't as upset as I was over the whole thing. I knew he was aware of how important this was for me. After all, I had spent my entire high school years preparing for this. I did not want to have braved Physics for nothing!

Things did turn around for me because a few weeks after I received another letter that came in the mail. It was congratulating me as there was now an opening for me and I was accepted to go to school. I was overjoyed. The Big Guy however, did not share my happiness. For a long time, I didn't understand why. I completed the requirements and even went to the school to go through with admittance.

The Big Guy went with me but I could tell he was not pleased at all. It just made no sense to me what so ever. Was I not supposed to go to college to be able to get a decent job? I wanted to be able to have a career I could be proud of. Mom had worked her whole life at jobs that went nowhere and had no real security. I wanted more than that for my life. I couldn't understand why the Big Guy was so dead against me going to that school.

The day started out bad enough when we walked into school so I could go through admittance. The longer we were there, the more aggravated the Big Guy got. He normally was not like that, so it really concerned me. I didn't not like this side of him at all. The more I went through with it, the ornerier he got. I tried to explain things, but he just wouldn't listen. I couldn't stand the way he was any longer. I had to do something, just wasn't sure what.

I remember meeting with an instructor and going on a tour of where I would be studying. I was so interested in it a million questions just started coming. It seemed like it was going to turn out fine and be just what I had wanted to do. Until he explained what I would be doing in my second semester that is. Remember I was expecting a baby and I was trying to plan everything out so I could do my studies and have a baby at the same time.

My heart dropped as he started to tell me what to expect. He said they didn't work with radiation and x-rays until the second semester. He said there were a number of different animals I would probably be working with and it included diagnosis with x-rays and there would most likely be a lot of it. That really changed my mind on the whole experience.

Since I was pregnant, I realized the importance of taking care of myself and not exposing myself to anything dangerous that would harm my unborn baby. I had promised myself I wouldn't do anything like that for 9 months for the sake of my babies' whole life. I would not risk the health of my child because I was learning something new and had to work with radiation. I knew what I had to do. I knew I had to decline the school until after the baby was born.

After thinking about what I was doing, my life would consist of a lot of changes. I would be a new wife going to a new school and about to be a new mother. I was sure I couldn't handle all that at the same time. Something would suffer because of it. I was so afraid it would be my baby because there was just too much for me to handle. I knew all three situations had its own stress. Mixing them could not be good for anyone let alone a new born baby.

I knew what I wanted to do, but I also knew what I had to do. The two were different. Mom would be so angry with me again, but when she calms down, I had hoped she seen the logic in my choice. There would be plenty of time for school after the baby was born. At least if I was able to go to this school, I wouldn't be risking anyone's health but my own. I refused to hurt my unborn baby because I was doing something I wanted. I had to put the baby first and me second from now on. I knew the Big Guy would understand.

Boy did he ever understand! He was so happy I decided on my own not to go to school. It was like talking to a different man. I could see the relief all over his face. Turned out it wasn't that he didn't want me to go on to school to learn something new. He didn't want me to go to school without him. He was afraid I would go away and meet someone new and not love him or want to be with him anymore. I couldn't believe he felt that way. Didn't the big dummy know how much I loved him? Did he forget how much I already gave up for him? Didn't he know that I'd rather pull my eyeballs out with a rusty spoon than leave him? Sometimes men are just thick headed!

After we talked, the Big Guy and I came to an understanding, things got better again between us. Not that it was bad, but the strain that was starting to grow disappeared. We were back totally to being together again. I knew I had a job cut out for me in explaining to my mother why I had decided not to go on to college as planned.

I really hoped she understood I was putting her grandchild's health above my wants and wishes. I was hoping she'd see what a sacrifice I was making. I'm not sure she ever did. I know she was very disappointed with me and kept saying I told you so over and over. It was like hearing a bad record you couldn't shut off. I knew I had time later to go to school. Why couldn't she see that as well? I had no answers for that question.

The only thing that happened that was positive besides being sure my baby would be healthy was it brought the Big Guy and I even closer together. It made me see how much I needed him even more. I knew there was a whole big world out there and I didn't think I had the courage to face it without him. I didn't want to be a part of anything that didn't include him. Nor did he want to be a part of anything that didn't include me. We are both still that way today.

After the problem with school was solved, preparations needed to be made for our wedding. I knew what I wanted and the Big Guy and I worked hard to get what we both wanted. I wanted a church wedding and I was going to have it. The Big Guy took on every job he could to help pay for things. We took trips into the city looking for everything we needed and wanted. This time in my life should have been fun putting all that stuff together, but it wasn't.

I was still fighting on and off again with my mom. She upset me so much. There would be times when I would listen to her holler at me and I would get mad, punch the wall and walk out. It was that or punch her but I couldn't do that. I still loved her and had great respect for her. After all, she was still my mother. I never told her about many things she caused. I didn't think it would help the situation.

The Big Guy and I still went on making our many plans. We still had high aspirations for our life. We needed to start as soon as possible. We tried to buy a better car. We found one real reasonable and went for it. We both knew we needed something that had better gas mileage if we were to survive. We went down to the local bank where I had my money and my savings account.

My mom banked there. The Big Guy had banked there for years. The Big Guy's family had banked there for years. We figured it would be no problem to get a loan. While talking to the banker, he told us he would love to give us the loan, but the Big Guy already had a small loan out he needed to pay off. If he paid that off, then we could get the loan.

I had more than enough money in the bank to pay

off such a small amount, so after much discussion, he agreed to pay the loan off with my money and then he'd pay me back. I told him I didn't want to be paid back because it would soon be our money and our loan. We went back down to the bank where I withdrew the money and paid off the loan. We walked back into the loan officer's office. He looked over the papers again and thanked us for paying off the loan so quickly.

He told us he did some talking with his boss and he needed to have a $600.00 down payment before he could give us a loan for the car. We told him we had to talk it over. We went back home again and discussed it more. I told him I had well over the $600.00 we needed. He didn't want to use my money at all. I again reminded him that it would be my car as well and I want to help pay for it. After more arguing, he agreed because we really did need that car. We went back to the bank.

The banker seemed surprised to see us back again and he was even more surprised to see the $600.00 cash sitting on his desk along with the loan papers. He took some time "reading" over the papers again. While we sat there watching him, I got the worst feeling. I tried to shake it off while I waited. He again thanked us for coming up with the down payment, but unfortunately, the Big Guy would need a co-signer.

I raised my hand and said, "I will co-sign for him. I have a steady job and I am not related to him." He very slowly looked at me for the first time. Maybe that is what bothered me so. He said in a very slow voice, "Okay, but you need your mother's permission." That statement hit me like a lead balloon. I can't tell you the anger I felt. My face must have shown my anger because as quick as I stood up to smack him, the Big Guy stood up faster and grabbed me.

I took the $600.00 back and said, "And then I guess you don't want my business anymore." I walked out into the lobby and withdrew all my money out of my savings and closed my account. It was not a lot of money, but it was enough. I would have taken out my CD's too, but they were not mature. I told the lady, when they were due, I would be back to get them as well. We walked out of that bank.

By the time we found a bank that would give us a loan, the car we wanted was already gone. So, we searched again for a car we could afford. We wanted something that would be good for a baby, yet get us where we needed to go. Everything was way out of our price range. We went to one dealer and found an old county squad car that was not in too bad of shape. We could afford it and the dealer promised he would give us almost what we paid for it in trade in when we could afford to get a better car. The new banker we found was willing to help so we were in business.

The "new" car was sure fast. It had bench seats that were vinyl. This was okay, but they were slippery. You had to wear your seat belt or else you'd slide all over the place. Sometimes it scared me, but the Big Guy was pretty happy with it. His brother who was on the fire department took it to go to a call one day. The Big Guy was telling him how fast the car was, so he jumped in our car because it was handy when the fire alarm rang.

He was warned to always use a seat belt, but I

don't think he listened to that part. Neither of us minded that he took it, as long as he got where he needed to go, helped out and then brought the car back, we were happy.

When he finally did bring the car back, he had a story to tell. He had gotten in the car and taken off so fast, he didn't take the time to put on his seat belt. He said he was gunning the car and then had to go around a corner. Before he could stop what was happening, he found himself sitting on the passenger side of the car. He had to scramble and try to pull himself back over to the driver's side before he wrecked the car. It could have turned out bad, but it didn't.

He was laughing as he was telling us about it and as we both imagined this big man sliding across the seat fighting to stay behind the wheel, we giggled at the picture it created too. I was just glad he wasn't hurt and I was glad he didn't wreck our car.

The Big Guy had already tested the speed and handling capabilities of the car. He had a buddy who was a cop. They used to hang out and had adventures together and did things that weren't exactly always on the legal side. Oh, it was nothing to hurt anyone or to do any major damage; it was just things that bent the laws a mite. They had helped each other out of many jams in the past and had a deep friendship and respect between them.

Anyway, the Big Guy was on the highway one day and realized he was following his buddy in his cop car. So, the Big Guy decided to play. He stepped on the gas and started to pass his buddy. Since there was no one coming towards him, he stayed alongside his buddy and waited for him to look over at him. When he did, he flipped him off and gunned the car and started a race.

Of course, his buddy couldn't pass him, but stayed on his bumper for a while. The next town was coming up and they both slowed down to make the turn off. When the Big Guy pulled over to talk to his buddy, he was questioned about what the heck he had under the hood. I guess he could have gotten arrested, but he was told to not do that again in a laughing kind of threat. They both laughed about it and it turned into a big joke between the two.

It wasn't until after we were married and the new baby came that I realized how wonderful it was to have a car like that. I know I'm jumping ahead in the story, but I have to tell you about that car. We were married, had the baby and were at his brother's house who was a couple of hours away visiting one weekend. His brother had older kids and I was constantly picking small things up off the floor as I was afraid my youngster would put these things in her mouth.

I guess I didn't do the best job, because I missed a coat pin. It was the same color as the carpeting and I didn't see it. Well, my baby did and in the mouth it went. I noticed she was breathing kind of funny and when I picked her up, I realized she was choking. I called to the Big Guy because I didn't know what to do.

His brother got to me first, grabbed the baby and just started shaking her. The Big Guy took her from him saying, "Let me have her." but there was not much he could do by himself. His finger was just too big. He did a baby Heimlich and would get the pin up in her throat where he could feel it, but his finger would push it back down again when he tried to get it out. He kept swearing and saying "I can't get it!"

Something kicked in with me and I told him, "Next time you work it up, let me try to take it out." My fingers were much smaller and I thought maybe I could get it out. The baby was still getting a little air, but the sound she was making was scaring the ever-loving God out of everyone. As soon as he looked at me and said, "I see it." I stuck my fingers in her mouth and felt the pin. I got my finger in behind it and pulled it out.

I can't tell you what a big relief that was! The baby was crying, but there was blood coming out of her mouth. We were all scared as we grabbed coats and a blanket to wrap around her and headed for our car. The Big Guy and I were both holding the baby and trying to calm her down, we told his brother to drive! Since he knew the area, we both thought that was best anyway. We were all packed in the front seat, so seat belts didn't really matter.

His brother gunned the car and raced to the hospital. On the way, the engine made a noise and a little smoke from under the hood started to appear. His brother says, "I think we blew a hose! What do you want do?" as steam started coming out from under the hood. I just looked at the Big Guy and he said, "It's only a car; we can get another, just get us there!"

So, we didn't stop until we pulled up to the hospital. We all ran in to get her looked at and was very relieved to find out the blood was just from a nick the pin made on the roof of her mouth. It bled worse than it really was. We were told she'd have a sore throat for a while, but she would be fine. I can't tell you the relief we all felt. That was the first time our children started scaring years off our lives.

I stayed with the baby while the Big Guy and his brother looked at the car. Sure enough, a water hose had broken. They went to the hardware store, bought another and replaced it. The car ran fine and was not hurt at all. I think if it were a regular car, it would have never made it to the hospital with a hose broken like that. The engine would have overheated and it would have been done for. At that moment, I loved that old car too.

Shortly after we brought that car home before we were married, another episode happened. I had a major argument with my mom and I ended up by storming out of the house very upset. I wanted to drive and get away for a while so I just took a road. It headed out of town and it wasn't a major highway, so I figured I'd be okay.

It was a curvy gravel road though; a road that didn't agree with the power of our new car. I thought I was driving okay, but the car started to fishtail around a sharp corner. I tried to steer out of it, but it was a pretty bumpy ride. I'm not exactly sure what happened, but I slammed on the brakes when I saw I was headed for a fence. It sure scared the tar out of me.

I drove back into town much slower and more careful. I went over to the Big Guy's house scared he was going to be angry with me. I walked in his house and found him in the basement. He took one look at me and knew something was wrong. I started to cry and could barely get out I wrecked the car. He asked if I was alright and for me not to worry because it was just a darn car. He tried hard to calm me down so he could get the whole story.

I told him what happened and where. He went outside to look at the car. The damage amounted to losing some of the trim, scratches and knocking the muffler system off the bottom of the car. He wanted to try to get the trim I lost so he took me back out where I said it happened. He could see where I started to fishtail and went off the road by the marks on the road.

I was so upset at the time; I didn't even know where I went. After I fishtailed and tried to steer out of it, I left the road and went up on a bank so steep that if I had been going slower, I probably would have rolled the car. It made him afraid I could have gotten hurt pretty bad and he was very glad I didn't.

He told me I had a new rule. From now on when I was mad, I was not to get behind the wheel of any car or truck. Mom never knew I almost got hurt really bad cause of how angry I was after a fight between her and I. I never told her pretty much because I didn't want to cause any harder feelings and because I didn't think she really cared anyway.

The damage to the car was pretty minimal and that was a good thing because we didn't have a lot of money to fix it. We had the wedding to pay for and I still didn't have a wedding dress. I wasn't sure what I wanted, but I knew I couldn't spend too much. I figured I would be able to spend around $100.00 on my dress. I know it wasn't much, but I was hoping I'd get lucky and find something nice at a second-hand store. We took trips every week or so into the city looking for things we wanted so it wasn't that far off track that I would run into something.

We had planned another trip to the mall. The Big Guy's folks and his brother were going to go with us. I invited my mom to ride along because I wanted to get the two families together to get to know each other. When mom told me, she didn't want to go, I begged her. She still refused saying she already had other plans. I was so disappointed.

We went anyway. After we got there, everyone went their own way. The Big Guy and I walked together down the mall just looking at things in the store's windows. As we look down the mall, we both saw a huge sale sign and white dresses. The Big Guy looked at me and asked if I wanted to look. I said, "Might as well while we are here." The dresses on the racks were pretty, but they were not my style. They just had too much lace. But they were in my price range. The most expensive dress was $79.00. I started to get excited to look. Maybe I would luck out and find my dress here.

A lady came out of the store and asked if we needed any help. We both told her we were looking for a wedding dress and did she have other styles. She said she had more inside the store. So, we followed her into the store. As we walked in, the Big Guy started to look at the racks of dresses. My gaze went straight to the back wall. I turned to him and told him to get out of the store. "NOW!"

He looked so surprised at me and started to protest. He was in the midst of asking why I wanted him to go; he wanted to help me look for a dress when I told him, no. He was not going to help me because he wasn't supposed to see my dress until our wedding day. That was one tradition I believed in. With everything that was already against us, I didn't want to hex our wedding before it even got a chance to get started.

As much as I wanted someone to be there with me as I picked out my wedding dress, I told him to go. He should find his mother and I would catch up with him later. He whined and tried to get me to let him stay, but I insisted. So, he sighed and acted like a defeated little boy and said, "Okay, I'm going." I swear I saw him pout as he walked away.

I waited a few minutes and asked the lady if he was gone yet. She looked and said he was. I was afraid he was hiding somewhere around a corner and the whole thing would be ruined because he would see which dress, I was looking at. He wasn't there, so I said, "Well, I want to see that dress." and I pointed up to the wall. She said she had a few of those and even had one in my size.

As she went to get it, I looked more at the dress. It was beautiful. It was an off the shoulder dress with just a little lace that lined the neckline and went down the dress at an angle and had lace around the bottom. I thought it was the most beautiful simple dress I ever saw. The clerk brought me the dress and it fit perfectly. It was just a little too long, which was the story of my life when I bought clothes. I told her I think my mom can help fix that. When I asked what the price was, I almost dropped my teeth. Remember my $100.00 limit? It was well under that. The whole dress was under $35.00 and that included tax!

I was so happy. The only thing I regretted was, my mother was not here when I tried it on or when I bought it. Even though I wanted her with me so bad; I couldn't pass it up and not buy the dress for that price. I paid for it and the lady put a dress bag on it to hide it. I wanted to be sure no part of the dress stuck out to keep it clean and to be sure the Big Guy wouldn't see it. I was so excited.

I walked all over the mall and looked for the Big Guy and his family. I found him with his mother. I asked her to go into the bathroom with me so I could show her the dress. The Big Guy looked like he wanted to go in to see it too, but he didn't say anything. His mom didn't think she should look as she felt my mom should be the first to see it.

I told her it was okay, because I really needed someone else's opinion if I bought the right dress or not. I knew my mom would be mad no matter what so I didn't think it mattered. She could not believe how pretty it was and the price was unbeatable. The Big Guy still whined he wanted to see the dress. I just gave him stern looks and his mom told him the dress sure was pretty and would be well worth the wait.

All the way home I dreaded walking into my house with that dress. I knew my mom would be angry I bought the dress without her. What could I do? I had begged her to go with but she didn't want to. I knew it would be hard to find a pretty dress on what little I had to spend.

When I found one so beautiful and so cheap, I couldn't leave it. I couldn't afford to drive back home to get mom to go back to get it. What if the dress was gone by the time we got back? I couldn't chance it. I would have to face her anger. At least I would have a beautiful wedding dress.

The moment I walked in the door holding the dress, I could see the look on mom's face. It had that disgusted look that said, "Okay, now what did you do?" The first words out of my mouth were, "Mom, I wanted you with when I bought my wedding dress, but I found this one and I couldn't pass it up." I showed mom the bill of sale. She looked at it and said, "Well if this is what you paid, the dress can't be much." She already had a bad attitude about the dress before she even seen it.

I opened the bag and showed her the dress. Her eyes popped out of her head and she exclaimed it was beautiful. I told her the length was a little too long when I tried it on, but it fit me great. She reassured me that was not a problem that it would be fixable and still couldn't believe such a beautiful dress was so cheap. I explained to her about the sale the whole store had on their dresses and how I lucked out finding it. It worked out anyway because I ended up by borrowing a one-bone hoop to wear under the dress which took care of the length problem. I didn't have to have a thing done to the dress.

I later went down to the local wedding store in town to see if they had a veil that would match my lace on my dress. They had one that wasn't too expensive and had matched pretty well. I paid more for the veil than I did the dress. The veil cost me $42.00. Since I was still under my limit, I thought I had done very well. I was very happy.

Exactly two weeks after I bought my dress, I

heard about it. Mom got mad at me for something she said I done again. In her anger, she added "It just wasn't right that you didn't want me along when you bought your wedding dress; that you preferred to have your mother-in-law there instead of me." I knew it was coming. The day I bought the dress I seen that writing on the wall before I even showed her the dress. As I said before, I could do nothing to please my mother. I'm not even sure why I kept trying.

The severity and frequency of our fights got so bad; I didn't even know if my mother would go to my wedding. She threatened so many times she wouldn't go I lost count of them. I really wanted her there, but she was so angry with me.

In my opinion it was too late to try to fix things with her. Too many things happened and too many hurtful things were said. I was knee deep in my life and there was nothing I could do about it. I couldn't have stopped it if I wanted to and I did not want to.

My mom and sister even tried to talk me out of marrying the Big Guy. They said I didn't have to get married to any man because of a child. There was always adoption or abortion. They said it didn't turn out so bad for me and my child would be okay too if I gave it up. And if things really got bad, I could end it before it got too far along. I was horrified. There was no way I was going to give up any child of mine.

There was no way I would ever kill a child either. I had enough mental problems due to being adopted, there was no way I was going make any child of mine go through the same thing. I don't think I could have lived with myself if I got an abortion. Besides, my baby was made out of pure love. There is nothing wrong with that.

No, I was going to get married and I was going to have and keep my baby no matter what. It didn't matter what pain I had to go through, or whatever I had to give up, I was going to do this. I figured the baby didn't ask to be born and I took the risk, so I should be grown up enough to deal with it as a responsible adult. I'm not sure that I was too responsible, but I was sure going to try.

The closer it got to the wedding, the more pressure we felt. Everyone was trying to tell us what to do and how we should do it. Plans would be made; people would hate it and disagree and plans would be changed. We knew what we wanted, but we had to remind everyone else it was OUR wedding and not theirs. We needed to get away and we needed to get away quick.

When the guys went to get fitted for their tuxes, I wanted to go along so I could see what they picked. The Big Guy was still a mite mad at me from the dress thing and refused to let me go. He said it would be bad karma if the bride seen the groom's outfit before the wedding day. I couldn't remember this rule, but he wouldn't listen. He was teasing me, but I didn't go. I whined about it too and we just had a laugh.

I reminded him, "No you still can't see my wedding dress!" He thought maybe he could make a deal with me. Sort of like I'll show you mine if you show me yours! I would not give in. I guess he was still worried about what my dress looked like. He knew what I paid for it and was sure it wasn't as nice of dress as what I deserved.

He was saving a thousand dollars in case I

needed it to buy a better dress. I had no clue he was saving that for me. I kept telling him my dress was beautiful and I was very happy with it. He gave me a look with his big blue eyes that again melted my heart and gave me a kiss. He told me he loved me. That was my most favorite thing to hear.

As he headed off with the guys to get their tuxes, he told me not to worry because even if he showed up wearing nothing but a speed-do, he'd make that stuff look good. I just laughed and told him, "I love you too, but you aren't getting married butt naked." and waited for him to come home.

He told me about what he did later after they got home. The guys took him out to dinner and drinks before they went to pick out the tuxes. Because of the number of guys renting tuxes, the Big Guy got his tux and shoes for free. He said he got his wedding dress cheaper than I got mine! As long as he wasn't going to show up buck naked, I was happy!

As bad as my mom hated the Big Guy, both his parents loved me. His mom treated me really good. She said she felt really bad about the way my mom was treating me. She didn't think it was right. I didn't deserve it in her opinion. To my surprise, she actually started treating me like one of her own daughters. I liked her a lot too. She was one nice lady. She was very hard working and took great pride in her house.

Don't get me wrong, she knew how to chew a person out when they deserved it and she could do it without any swear words, but she had a big heart. I remember the Big Guy saying his mom had a sharp tongue and could make you feel lower than the belly of a snake when she had a mind to. I sure didn't want to make her mad at me that's for sure.

I would try to help her out any chance I got. His dad seemed to like me too. For what reason, I didn't know because I was too afraid to really talk to him much. He just scared me and I didn't want to be alone with him. Not that I thought he would hurt me; I was just afraid I'd say the wrong thing and make him angry or make him not like me. The Big Guy always said his dad loved me more and thought more of me than he ever thought of him.

The Big Guy was the black sheep of the family. He could never seem to do anything right in his dad's eyes. He thought dating and marrying me was the first thing the Big Guy ever did right. I was just glad he liked me and since I was going to be a part of his life it sure made things easier. I had to take his family along with the package deal. I didn't mind. I had a small family and I thought having a big family for a change would be great.

I was just glad there was someone who was not down on us getting married. Not that I felt it was a mistake, it was just depressing to have to fight for our love all the time. I would have fought more if it was needed, but it would have been nice not to fight at all. Not only did I gain the Big Guy's immediate family, the number of his aunts, uncles and cousins on both sides are so huge, there is no way I could keep them all straight much less remember them all. After the wedding if someone asked me if I was related to someone with the same last name, I said, "Probably." without really knowing who they were talking about. They were all related anyway so it didn't matter.

I had no clue just how much my life was changing

when I married the Big Guy. I was not sure I was ready for it. He loved me more than life itself and I knew I wouldn't be alone ever again. That felt so good because I loved him more than life itself. To have love returned with the same energy it is given is such a good thing. I knew even then our love would out last anything. With him by my side, I knew I could do anything.

The wedding was coming closer and closer. The pressures got hotter and hotter. It was late summer and the heat was terrible. A few weeks before the wedding and while I was standing in church wearing shorts and a nice top, I got so hot and uncomfortable. I just didn't know how I was going to stand at the alter in that dress in this heat. I prayed for cooler weather.

During that mass, mom leaned over to me and commented on the pretty guitar music that was playing. I couldn't tell her who it was because I knew she wouldn't like it. She didn't find out it was the Big Guy playing until she went up for communion. When she walked across the front of the church and looked up into the choir loft, she saw the Big Guy sitting there playing his guitar, I saw the look on her face and I knew she was mad. It went from a happy smile to an angry scowl in 1 second flat. Was there nothing about the Big Guy that made her happy? I don't know why she was so hard on the Big Guy, but she was.

She shouldn't have been so down on him. He was not that bad of a guy. Actually, she never knew, but during his last year of high school, he actually thought of going to school to become a Catholic priest. He had been an altar boy throughout his whole life and he knew the church well. He had an interest in it, but when he realized he would not be allowed to marry and have a family, he decided the priesthood was not for him.

After high school, he tried to go to college for electrical engineering, but he couldn't get the funding to go. The school told him he was pretty much out of luck and not to expect an opening until second semester of next year. He was so disappointed and really needed to do something with his life. He was dating a lady at the time who had two kids from a previous marriage. He thought he loved her and had asked her to marry him. He thought he was ready to be a husband and a dad to those kids. He got along with the daughter, but the son as a different story. They seemed to rub each other the wrong way and didn't get along at all.

Since he couldn't find a steady job, he went to enlist in the army. He wasn't 100% sure he was doing the right thing. Because he needed a job and he figured if she was true to him while he was gone, it would be right. If she wasn't, then he would think things out and deal with it then. Deep down I think he was running away to clear his head so he could do the right thing.

After he raised his hand, the school had contacted him letting him know they had a spot open and he could go to school. It was too late because he was already sworn in the Army. The Army wouldn't let him out of his promise and he was stuck. It wasn't long after that when he left to begin his army career.

The priest had found out the Big Guy was coming home on leave one weekend and for a joke put him down as an altar boy. The Big Guy found out about it and to show the priest he still cared, he showed up and served for mass. The priest was surprised to see him and said he didn't expect him to serve.

The Big Guy told the priest, he figured if Jesus sacrificed his life for him; then he could sacrifice one Sunday for Jesus. Then he told the Priest about how he sang in the church choir on the base for something to do on the weekends. The priest was surprised the Big Guy continued his church habits even after he left town. Yes, he had ties to the church and was not a total bad guy after all.

Mom would have been happy to know that if the Big Guy would have continued on with his promise to swear off all women, we probably would have never gone as far as we did. Just before we met, the Big Guy was so upset with women; he said he didn't want anything serious to do with them ever again.

While he was gone, his mom would write and tell him about what was happening while he was away. She told him of how she heard his fiancée was not being true to him. He didn't take it to heart because he didn't think his mom liked her anyway and wanted them to break up. It wasn't until after his best friend wrote and told him the same thing when he started believing it.

After he got home and realized she had cheated on him, he became angry. She had done so much to him while he was gone. He had sent money home for her to make his car payments and she didn't do it. She spent the money on herself and her kids and didn't pay his bills for him. When he got home, he was so far behind; he had to sell his car in order to get current. He was not happy with that at all.

Besides in finding out she really did cheat on him; he knew he couldn't stay with her. She made him angry one day shortly after he got home, he had enough and out the door he walked. The only thing she was concerned about was the trailer they were living in because he had paid half of the cost. Instead of fighting with her, he let her have it all. He just took his things he wanted and let her have the rest. When he met me, he was still very angry with all women.

He even told me he fought falling in love with me. He admitted he would sit up late at night just thinking about it and he would tell himself he really didn't want to be with any woman. He promised himself he would take it slow to be sure it truly was love and not just lust again. He didn't want to jump in the sack with me right away and rush things. Time would be needed to be completely sure it was true love.

If he had been stubborn and kept to that promise of not being with any woman, he would not have stuck around me to see if it was love or not. He probably would have treated it like another one-night stand and then he would have left me. See how a rash decision would have changed things forever?

It was the weekend before the wedding. We decided to take a trip just to get away before we were driven nuts. A trip north to see my sister and maybe go camping was the ticket to some relief. Whatever we did, we needed a break. I worked nights and we decided to leave when I got off work at midnight. Our bags were packed and as soon as I walked out of work, we took off. I was so tired but that was okay. It felt so good to be leaving; it wasn't long before I fell asleep in the seat.

I don't know how long I slept, but I woke up to being slammed into the car door one second and slammed into the Big Guy's side the next. As I struggled to sit up, I asked him what the heck was he doing. He replied, "I'm trying not to hit this huge herd of deer!" They were out all over the road and he knew he'd hit some of them for sure if he tried to slow down. Our car handled the movements just fine, as that's what it was built for.

Remember I told you about the car's vinyl seats? They were the kind that if you didn't wear a seat belt, you were in trouble. The seats were so slippery. I always hated it because whenever I was upset with the Big Guy for whatever reason and didn't want to sit next to him, all he had to do was turn a corner real fast and I slid right into him.

My normal spot was sitting in the middle next to him. I would move closer to the door to let him know I was upset and I'd be danged if he wouldn't turn a corner fast to slide me right back against him. I guess I should have put on a seat belt, but I never thought about doing that.

I couldn't stay mad at him for long, but it was very aggravating. That night I was lying in the seat trying to sleep and sliding all over while he was zigzagging through the herd of deer. At least he didn't hit any of them. I felt good about that. He came close to hitting one a time or two, but he got through the herd pretty safely.

We got to my sister's house pretty early that morning and was able to nap for a bit. After we got up again, we went to a store and bought groceries so we didn't impose on anyone. My sister's mother-in-law said we didn't have to, but that's the way the Big Guy was. He didn't like to take anything from anyone that he didn't pay for.

We had a good time with my sister's mother-in-law. She was a fine lady and fun to be around. We had a lot of laughs and even did some fishing and swimming. I was glad we got away until we got a call from home. My mom had found out they were hiring a janitor at the school and was upset because the Big Guy wasn't there to see about getting the job. She wanted to know why we left town and why we were mooching off of my sister.

This made me really angry because number one, the Big Guy already had an interview and was told he was their second choice and they had already hired who they wanted. Number two, we had bought all the food for the weekend and we were not mooching off of anyone. She was just mad because we were not home and I might be happy for a little while.

She even called the Big Guy's mother and raked her over the coals about it. His mother told her to keep her dang nose out of our business and to leave us alone. I don't think Mom liked that but it must have made the Big Guy's mom feel good to say it.

After that, even my brother-in-law made me mad. He took me out for a bike ride to get me alone to try to talk me out of marrying the Big Guy. He had been working on his bike and when he was done, he asked me if I wanted to ride with him to test drive it. He wanted to be sure he had it fixed. He wasn't worried about it breaking down because he wasn't going far. I agreed because I liked to ride. I didn't know he wanted to talk with me much less what the conversation would be about.

We stopped in a little bit at a nearby bar and he started in on me. He told me I didn't need to marry the Big Guy just because I was expecting and I had other options. I really didn't want to hear it, so I told him to forget it that my mind was set. I was marrying the Big Guy if he liked it or not!

When we got back to the house, he noticed the lug nut that held the back wheel on was loose. I remember him laughing saying we could have been hurt bad. The Big Guy was not happy at all once he knew that and told me he never wanted me to ride with him ever again. He was even madder when I told him what my brother-in-law had to say.

Man, I wish people would just leave us alone. The relief we felt was replaced with anxiety not only because of the opposition we faced but because we knew the next week would be the longest week of our life.

Chapter 11

Before we made it to the alter, there were several times when I thought I lost the Big Guy. I was so amazed I found anyone who loved me as much as he did, I was constantly doubting the fact he really did love me. I had always thought there is no way I will ever find anyone in this whole world that would ever care and love me more than life itself.

I kept pinching myself to see if it was really true and I kept waiting for him to say he changed his mind and walk away. The Big Guy had promised he'd never leave me, ever. So far, he is still with me, but still today, I sometimes wonder if I will ever hear that slamming of the door.

The first time I really was scared about making the Big Guy angry enough to tell me to hit the road was one night late after work. It was in the winter months meaning it was pretty dang cold. The Big Guy let me take his truck to work so I wouldn't have to walk home. I was happy for it as I was late going to work that day. The Big Guy's truck was a 1975 GMC Jimmy. It was his baby. From what I was told, he hardly let anyone drive his truck, so I considered myself privileged to be able to drive it.

Apparently how the story went, he had a white

Camaro that was pretty fast. He let his little brother drive it once and by the time it was returned, the tires were spun off. His brother had raced it around town, smoking the tires, peeling out and driving pretty wildly in the city limits.

The Big Guy got yelled at by several adults for driving his car that fast in town because they recognized his vehicle. He even got reported to the police. The Big Guy was pretty angry at his brother and besides that, his brother never replaced the tires he ruined. So, after that, he just never let anyone else drive his vehicles.

I told you his truck was his baby. He never drove it hard. It was always clean as a whistle on the outside. The inside was not real clean, but was not too bad for a guy. He worked hard to pay for it, so he never beat it, he respected it. When he took the truck off road, he always drove it carefully. It was a pretty cool truck.

It was blue in color. The truck had a 4-inch lift kit in it, so it sat up higher than a normal truck. I was amazed the Big Guy let me drive it, so when I did, I was always careful. He said he always laughed when he saw me in it. The truck had big captains' chairs in the front that sat up high. I was glad for that because it was easier for me to see the road over the huge hood.

The Big Guy said I looked so funny driving it. According to him, I looked like this tall woman driving the truck, but when I got out and walked around it, my head didn't even go up past the hood. I of course, didn't see any humor in this, but he sure did. All I can say is I was sure glad the thing had running boards! I'd a never got up in it by myself. I got teased a lot because of my height and this didn't help the situation either. I didn't mind him doing the teasing because it was never mean and I could tease him right back.

Driving the truck was pretty fun. I don't know if you recall what this model looked like, but the roof was detachable. In the summer it was like driving a convertible with an attitude when it would be hot enough to take the roof off. It was pretty cool to show up at picnics at the lake in it with the top off.

I loved it. I learned a lot with that old truck. I learned you always wanted to vacuum it out before you drove it after taking the top off. It had been a long winter and a beautiful spring when we decided it was warm enough for the top to be off.

I had asked the Big Guy about cleaning it out and he said it would be okay. Well, I should have at least brushed it out. The cloud of dust and dirt that came out of it was terrible. We laughed and choked and sputtered all the way to the next town. When we started down the highway and the cloud started rising, the Big Guy assured me it wouldn't be long before it was blown away. Man, was he wrong! So, let that be a lesson. Clean out your truck or car before putting the top down!

The day of my senior picnic, the Big Guy planned to pick me up after wards. He had the top off the jimmy and he had my new pup with him. He was hungry, so we went to get some fast food. He got a hot ham and cheese and a turkey club and since he insisted, I get something too, I got a mushroom and Swiss burger.

I tried to tell him I wasn't all that hungry, but he wanted to be sure I ate. I remember we were talking and laughing as we picked up our food. Since we had the pup, we decided to eat in his truck. She was sitting on the floor between the seats smelling the food and wondering what was up.

The Big Guy shared a couple of bites with her of the hot ham and cheese. That was fine with her as she liked it okay. When she smelled that turkey club, it was a whole different story. It was like she grew 10 times her size as she scrambled up to his lap to try to get at that sandwich. She wanted it so bad!

The Big Guy was driving at the time and it was not easy to hold the truck on the road, try to keep the sandwich safe in one hand and the dog in the other. I was laughing at the site of it as I tried to hold the pup back. I couldn't seem to get a good hold on her as she wiggled out of my grasp just to try to get the sandwich again.

We couldn't get over how intense she was at getting that food. It was so funny because how hard should it be to try to control a pup that little. She was really bound and determined to get that sandwich! Turned out, she really had a weakness for turkey or chicken. She liked turkey the best and Thanksgiving was her day of the year! She made sure none of each year's bird went to waste after that!

I remember parking the truck pretty fast that fateful day he let me drive it to work; turning it off and running for the door of the plant. I was almost late and I wanted to get punched in on time. I made it just in the nick of time and went into work. I didn't think any more about the truck until after my shift when I left to go home. I had stayed later than I normally did on a school night because I was trying to make extra money.

By the time I got back out to the truck, it was pretty cold. I put the key in and tried to turn the key to warm the truck. I say try because the durn thing wouldn't turn. I became so scared! All I could think of, was, "Oh no, what did I do to his truck?!" I retraced my actions before work and for the life of me I could not think of what I did wrong. I checked the position of the shifter and tried to turn the key again.

Nope, it still wouldn't turn. I got out of the truck and had to go back in to the building to call the Big Guy. I was so scared! As soon as he answered, I was apologizing right away. I kept saying, "I'm sorry, I broke it, you're going to be mad! I didn't mean it!"

He stopped me and asked what the heck I was talking about. I told him; I couldn't get the key to turn in his truck. He started to laugh and said I wasn't to worry about it. I was calming down long enough to hear him ask me to collect all the extension cords I could get my hands on. He was going to call his buddy to come down and help thaw out his truck.

Turned out, he had loaned his truck to the Kempo instructor earlier that day. There was so much snow; the instructor needed a 4-wheel drive to get water out to his horses. For some reason, he decided to fill the water cans inside of the cab with the hose. The hose got away from him and sprayed down the whole steering column. It soaked the whole thing.

Of course, the Big Guy didn't tell me about it before I took it to work. The water froze in the column and that's why nothing would turn. The plan was to bring a space heater down, heat it up and thaw it out so the truck could be started.

I walked around the plant grabbing every extension cord that wasn't already in use and had quite an armful to take out to the truck. After I got back out there, I saw the Big Guy sitting in the driver's seat with his hands in his lap and his head down. I knew something was wrong.

While I was in gathering the cords, he ran down and tried to turn the key. It didn't turn, so he got a little mad and palm struck the key to maybe break the ice. The key and the ignition switch sheared off and was in his hand in pieces.

That made him even angrier. You know that lock that keeps the shifter in place when a vehicle is not running? Well, he grabbed the shifter and yanked it completely down. It now bounced and wouldn't stay in place anymore. He got even madder. That lock that keeps the steering wheel from moving when the vehicle is not running? He grabbed the steering wheel with both hands and twisted it breaking the column. The steering wheel now spun around in many circles.

I was amazed at the strength the Big Guy showed that night. He did all of this in a sitting position. I asked him if he felt better now and I told him, "Well, we don't need these extension cords no more." I turned and went back in the building to return the cords.

I ran into my supervisor and was asked what I was doing and if we got our truck running alright. I said, "No it isn't going to be running tonight." I told him what had happened and he didn't believe me. I told him to go out and see for himself as the truck would be there until it was towed away.

My supervisor walked out with me. The Big Guy had the window rolled down and was still sitting in the driver's side looking at all the damage he had done. The supervisor stuck his head in the window and looked at the sheared off key and switch in his hand, took his finger and spun the steering wheel. While it was still spinning, he watched as the Big Guy bounced the shifter. His eyes bugged out and he swore under his breath. He just looked at me, shook his head and turned and walked away without saying a word.

Later after having the truck towed away, we found out it took over 375 pounds of pressure to break each and every one of those locks on that column. I was so amazed! I told the Big Guy getting angry like that solved nothing as now the column had to be replaced in his truck. It was an expense he didn't need. I know he felt terrible about doing it, but it created a new appreciation my supervisor and others had for him.

It was the first time he really showed me what body strength he possessed. That story has also helped me out a time to two in the past. Whenever I had any unwanted attention from another man, I would tell that story. I called it my Jimmy story.

Guys that were giving me trouble and who would not leave me alone usually got a weird look on their face as they walked away from me as fast as they could after hearing that story. It sure came in handy at times when I needed it.

Another time I was sure the Big Guy would never want to see me again was one night after we were done playing in the pit orchestra for a play. The play was Oklahoma. A lady who was in charge of the production knew we were musicians and asked if we'd like to play. It was another chance to play music together, so we agreed.

We had to spend time practicing the music, so for us it killed two birds with one stone again. My mom couldn't complain about us being together this time because we really had no choice.

The big opening night was here and I was so excited. Of course, because of work, I was later than I wanted to be. The Big Guy was already there; I was to meet him. As I was driving up the street looking for a parking place, some girl stepped out to cross the road in front of me.

Always happens when you're in a hurry; I stopped, she stopped. I tried to go, she tried to go. It was very aggravating especially since I was already close to being late; I stopped dead in the street and motioned her across. After she cleared the front of my car, I stepped on the gas.

The tires were a mite bald and as much power that old squad had; it didn't take much to squawk the tires. The cop that seemed to have it in for the Big Guy was behind me. He knew the car and thought the Big Guy was driving. He turned on the lights and followed me right quick. Since I was in a hurry, I didn't pay much attention to who was behind me. I went around the block and parked in the grocery store parking lot which was not too far from the theater.

I jumped out of the car and went straight to the back seat to get my bass out without looking anywhere else. As I was struggling with my bass, I happen to glance over my shoulder, I saw the cop getting out his night stick and walking towards the car. He stopped quick when he realized it was me and not the Big Guy. I could see his partner sitting in the passenger side shaking his head with his hand over his face.

The cop was aggravated with me for squawking the tires. He says, "You're a little heavy on the gas, aren't you?" I told him I was sorry, but I was late for the play. I didn't mean to squawk the tires. I told him the tires were pretty bald and they would probably squawk no matter how fast I was going. He told me to watch it and I should get new tires.

This was just a warning for me to slow down and he said he would be watching for me. I just couldn't believe he was actually getting out his night stick. If it were the Big Guy, he probably would have taken it way and beaten him to death with it. Funny how cops don't think of things like that isn't it.

I walked into the theater under stern looks. I quickly apologized and sat down next to the Big Guy after setting up my bass. I wasn't too late, but late enough. I quietly told the Big Guy about the run in with the cop and he laughed. I didn't think it was funny, but he did. I just chocked it up to the Big Guy being who he was.

The Big Guy had brought his fiddle down to the theater with him. He said he thought it would be good to have an extra in case the lady who played the violin broke a string. She thanked him for his thoughtfulness and looked at the fiddle. It was pretty, but didn't have a great sound. It was kind of tinny sounding. I could hear it and you could tell the lady thought so too by the way she quickly returned it to its case.

Thankfully, she didn't need it that night. We played pretty well and everyone was happy with the music. After the play was over and after the crowd left, the Big Guy and I decided it was time for us to leave as well. He carried my bass because it was heavier and his guitar. I carried the fiddle.

The case that belonged to the fiddle was an older one. It was in pretty good shape, but the latch was something else to be desired. It didn't click, but was just a hook that latched into a hoop. It wasn't tight and would flop open pretty easy. The Big Guy warned me to be careful as I carried the fiddle. I thought I was carrying it with the open side to my leg in case it flopped open. I thought it was alright.

I was wrong. He asked me where I parked the car and after telling him, we started to walk. We were almost to where I had parked the car when it happened. The case flopped open and the fiddle fell out onto the blacktop of the parking lot. I was mortified. The fiddle broke into a million pieces it seemed.

I immediately looked at the Big Guy with an open mouth telling him I was so sorry! He had this look I didn't want to see on his face. I helped him find and pick up every piece. He started to tell me it was the lock's fault and not mine, but I knew better. I felt so horrible. My heart sunk. I knew for sure he'd hate me forever. I knew that was a crime that had no forgiveness. I broke a very delicate instrument. It was all my fault and there was no way I could make it better. The Big Guy didn't say much, as I knew he was angry. I didn't stay long at his house that night because I felt so terrible.

I know that my tears didn't help the whole thing. The Big Guy hated it when I cried, so I think that's why he was not as hard on me as he should have been. I couldn't help but cry the whole way home and long into the night. I was so sure he never wanted to see me ever again after that.

That was one sleepless night. I had never felt so terrible. All I could think of was he hates me. I ruined everything. All that had happened was gone in one fell swoop of a smashed fiddle. I tossed and turned all night long. I dreaded the morning when I would go over to the Big Guys house like normal. He had told me he wasn't mad, but I could see different. I knew for sure the next time I seen him; he would tell me he had enough. For all the trouble and heartache, I made him go through this would be the last straw. I didn't know what to do.

The next morning came even though I didn't want it to. I got up like usual and went over to his house. As I walked in the front door, I asked his mom where he was because he wasn't upstairs in his room like normal. She told me he was down in the basement and had been there for a long time. I reluctantly went down the stairs afraid of what I would find.

At least he would be telling me he wanted to break up in private. When I got to the basement, his back was to me. He was working with something on the bench. As I got to him, I could see it was the fiddle. He looked at me and smiled and instantly gave me a hug and a kiss. He was not angry at all.

He had stayed up all night working on putting that fiddle back together. He had glued, sanded and stained it back to being in once piece again. The poor thing was beautiful! The only mark it had was on the end where it smacked the pavement. I was disappointed in myself, but he told me not to worry because the marks just gave it character.

He said he tried hard to sand the road rash out of it, but it was in too deep. Other than that mark, I thought it looked better than it did before. The finish didn't look as tinny. It had a softer look to it; the kind of look that comes from wood that was well taken care of. The grains showed and it was pretty. He was happy with his work even though he hadn't slept at all. He was tired but he said the work was well worth it.

I kissed him and hugged him as tight as I could. I again apologized and asked him if he was sure he didn't hate me. I told him I'd understand if he wanted to break up and hate me forever. He laughed and called me silly. He said he loved me more than any piece of wood. I can sure tell you I was so relieved. I felt so much better. As I remember the fiddle hitting the ground, I still shed a tear, but then I remember how beautiful he made it and I smile.

Later that night as we went down to the theater again for the second showing of the play, he took the same fiddle. Turns out that lady broke a string on her violin and actually needed the Big Guy's fiddle. She couldn't believe it was the same one. She wouldn't believe it. As she played it and we listened to the beautiful sounds that came out of it, you could tell it wasn't the same fiddle.

After the Big Guy told her the story of me breaking it and him staying up all night putting it back together, she was amazed. "The tone," she said "Is so sweet and so much better than what it was before." She didn't know why it was so different, but I did. It's because the first time it was just made. The second time it was put together, it was put together with love. Love makes one heck of a difference in everything.

We used to do a lot together. I suppose you could say I had a lot of firsts with the Big Guy. There were a lot of things we did that could have ended badly I guess, but nothing ever did. Now, don't go thinking naughty. Because you're not going to hear about that stuff. That is pretty personal and it is just between me and the Big Guy. Although he would love to brag about things, I never will because I don't think that is proper. Anyhow, the firsts I'm talking about include camping, fishing, driving and guns.

I never got much chance to do any of those things when I was a kid. Mom's boyfriend did take us fishing every now and then and I loved it, but I didn't get to do it as much as I wanted. I remember him promising we'd go on a certain day and waiting and waiting for him. Oh, he'd show either when it was too late or the next day and he'd always have an excuse like, it was too windy or it was too wet to go.

Let me tell you as a kid, you don't care about those things. All you want to do is to be able go like it was promised. It never mattered if you caught anything, but it was just the fact of going. When you didn't go because of whatever reason, it was nothing but a letdown.

The Big Guy and I spent a lot of time going fishing. Anything we did outside was just fine with me. It started with him taking me hunting for the first time. I had no knowledge of guns nor did I want to learn. I had seen Bambi as a youngster and with my love for animals, I thought guns were the most fearful and terrible things there were. I couldn't believe I actually agreed to go deer hunting with the Big Guy.

All I did was dress in orange and go along for the ride. I walked were I was told and did what I was told. I was too afraid of making any mistakes. I did enjoy being out in the woods with the Big Guy. When I realized I had actually had fun, I decided maybe hunting wasn't so bad after all.

The Big Guy hunted and used the meat, so it was for a reason and had a use. The Big Guy never shot anything for the fun of it, he ate everything he killed. Besides he didn't make me shoot anything, so I was good with it.

When it got nice enough to spend more time outside, we'd go fishing. When we didn't go fishing, the Big Guy wanted to go out and shoot guns. Target shooting, he called it. I was all raring to go fishing, but I couldn't say the same for this target shooting. I was scared to death of guns and just didn't know if I would like that at all. I would tell him how scared I felt and he would laugh and he would urge me to try anyway.

He would say, "You don't know if you like it until you try it." Since I wanted to please him, I agreed. He took me to the local rifle range and set me up with his rifle which was only a 22 caliber. It was a pretty gun with a wood stock and had a deer rifle's scope mounted on it. He showed me how to load it and told me what the rules were at the range. After we set up some targets, I was in business. He let me alone while he went to the longer range to shoot his deer rifle which was a bigger caliber.

I started plinking away with the rifle and I couldn't believe what I was doing! It was actually a lot of fun! I was shooting at paper targets, pop cans and empty shot gun shells he sat on the fence. I was knocking them down left and right. I'm not sure how many shells I went through, but I know it was a lot.

His little brother went too and was angry because I was shooting better than he was. He was complaining that I was using a scope and he wasn't and that was why I was shooting better. I thought what a baby! I didn't really care because I was just having fun. It didn't matter to me if I hit the target or not. I was learning something new and enjoying it.

The Big Guys little brother was still whining about not shooting very good when the Big Guy walked up and heard him. He started teasing him saying, "What's wrong, mad cause a girl is beating you?" I giggled which did not help matters much. He complained again about the scope.

The Big Guy told him it didn't matter; you could shoot or you couldn't. The scope didn't do a thing but make the target more visible. He proved the point by pulling out his pistol and hitting seven shot gun shells sitting on the fence with 6 shots. His brother was miffed and said, "That was just luck, I bet you can't do that again!" So, I went and put the shells back up again and the Big Guy hit seven shells again with six shots. His brother never went shooting with us again. I didn't mind that at all.

According to the Big Guy, women are better at shooting guns naturally. He says that a woman's strength is in her legs and hips and not in her arms and shoulders. A woman doesn't try to overpower a gun which allows the gun to move like it was meant to be.

A man will try to control or man handle a gun which hampers its effects. The Big Guy knew what he was talking about as he was a weapons specialist in the Army. He had to learn about all weapons. As far as I was concerned, I shot okay and liked to do it. As far as his brother was concerned, he couldn't hit the broad side of a barn standing inside it. It didn't bother me any as I tried not to make too much fun of him. He was pretty good at making a fool of himself anyway.

There were other times when we would go out to this tree farm the Big Guy used to work at. He worked there when he was younger and planted countless trees. A new owner had it but his friend still had some access, so we would go with him from time to time. There was a shooting range already set up and I liked the place immensely.

The friend was the janitor from school that I told you about. He was a real nice guy, a little weird but very pleasant to be around. He would look at me like he wanted to ask what was a nice girl like me doing with an oaf like the Big Guy, but he never asked it. We liked hanging around him because he was fun and because the jokes flew freely between the two.

The range was set up with close targets and far

away targets. It had old bowling pins suspended by wires to shoot at. It was real fun to pick your target and make the pin move. The Big Guy was a good shot, however and would easily get bored with the simple targets. Instead of aiming at the pin, he would aim at the wire holding the pin.

After cutting all the wires before his friend could get a shot off, he would get mad and say, "Okay, you big jerk, now you can walk your backside down there and put them all back up again!" You could tell he was aggravated, but the Big Guy would tease him and we'd all end up by laughing. Yea, he was a pretty good guy.

The janitor's mom was a heck of a lady. We loved to go to their house to visit with her. She was 100% Swedish and man did she have an attitude. She was like in her eighties, I'm not really sure how old she was, but she was old. She was a feisty old lady that made me laugh. She wasn't afraid to tell anyone anything. If she seen it and felt it, she said it. I loved her for that.

There was this other guy who was big and tall and was pretty much a mooch that liked to go there for coffee and conversation as well. He was another friend of the Big Guy. I was okay with him, but there was something about him I didn't like. He seemed to have a pretty big mouth and I was not sure if that was it or if it was something different that I didn't like. I never figured it out.

One day, after it snowed, we drove by her house. We saw the sweet old lady out there shoveling her snow. We stopped and the Big Guy took the shovel away from her. She insisted that she should shovel, but he just said, "No, you go in and make me a cup of coffee, I'll finish the walk."

She wouldn't let go of the shovel at first. The Big Guy would laugh and tell her she didn't want to make him put an old lady's head in the snow bank now, did she? She knew of course he was only kidding, but after putting her hand on the side of his face and looking in his eyes, she would smile at him and go inside to make her coffee. The Big Guy really loved the daylights out of that old lady!

Now when I say make her coffee, I mean make her coffee. It was not just putting coffee grounds in a filter, adding water and waiting for an automatic drip either. She had a regular peculator that when she made her coffee, it took at least a half an hour or more to make. If your saying why wait that long for just a cup of coffee, let me tell you, it was well worth the wait.

I don't know how she did it, but I do know she used an egg to make it with. Something about when the egg was cooked and floated to the top, it took the grounds with it and it was done. I know she strained it too because she didn't want any grounds to be left in it at all. It was THE best cup of coffee I had ever had.

The old lady was a baker in her younger days. She worked for a bakery down in Chicago and man, did she know how to bake. She made this jelly roll that you would die for. If she offered to make it you would ask which country, she wanted invaded and what did she want brought back. It was that good.

When the Big Guy was still shoveling, this loud mouth guy would come in and walk right past him without helping or even offering to help. There would even be a second shovel just sitting there, but he never touched it but maybe once. He would normally come in and sit at the table, talk and wait for the coffee and jelly roll. I would always laugh because when she served it and he reached for it first, she would slap his hands and say, "My Big Guy gets it first, you did no work!" I would try not to giggle too loud, but it always tickled me.

Yes, she was all Swedish. She had that broken talk to match. You could understand her alright but at times, she would revert back to her original language. When her and her son got together every now and then they would argue about something. I never knew what the argument was about. Maybe it was something she didn't like, I don't know. You just knew they were arguing because it would always sound heated and it would always be in Swedish.

Once, her son said something to her the Big Guy didn't like. The language was similar to German and since he understood it a little, he told him quite sharply not to talk to his mother that way. He even cuffed him up side his head when he said it. His mother just looked at the Big Guy and smiled at him. His friend just turned and asked if he really understood that.

The Big Guy's grandfather had talked to him in German when he was a little boy. He may not be able to speak, but he can understand a few things when he hears it. The Big Guy told him what he said and his friend told his mom they would have to be careful what they said from now on around the Big Guy.

When they argued, you just knew she would win

too because every argument always ended with her walking way with a huge smile on her face and him saying in disgust, "Awww Ma!"

It was funny and he'd always have a grin on his face because he knew no matter what there was no way he could ever win. Neither the Big Guy or I would have to say, she won again huh? But we would say it anyway just to kid him about it. He'd just shake his head and say something in Swedish and we'd all laugh. Yea, I loved that old lady!

I had a lot of respect for the janitor as well. I liked the way him and the Big Guy talked. It was never anything that was a put down. It was always no nonsense and straight to the point. I appreciated his straight talk and listened to what he had to say. He never once said we shouldn't be together. He would just talk facts so we would know what we were facing. It was refreshing.

I respected him so much; I even asked him if he'd walk me down the aisle if my mom didn't show up. He was very flattered and said he would if it came to that. He did want to know if I minded if he took pictures of the wedding. I said of course he could take all he wanted.

Another one of our favorite pastimes was discovered while we were fishing. We were out at the local lake that was right near a golf course. The Big Guy actually lived on the golf course in an apartment so it was really close. We'd borrow his brother's canoe and paddle all over the lake. Now the lake looks deep, but after being on it in a canoe, we found out it wasn't very deep at all. Matter of fact, many places we would drag the bottom.

On one of these trips, we noticed stray golf balls on the bottom of the lake. Many a golfer would lose his golf balls at various points on the course. The ball would land right in the water and there was no way the golfer would go after it. We decided we could gather the lost balls and maybe make some extra cash by cleaning them up and selling them back to the golfers.

It worked out pretty well. The only time we had a problem was when we'd run across the occasional ball that had initials on them. The owner would claim them and not want to pay for it. You'd think they'd be willing to pay something after all; it was our feet that was in that cold lake recovering them and then cleaning them up. People will be people and we made enough for it to be worthwhile. I just never expected to ever be knee deep in the lake in mid-May.

Canoeing on the lake was beautiful and we enjoyed it a lot. We got to see angles of the lake that normally we couldn't see. One time we noticed a goose on a nest out in the middle of the lake. There was a little island that used to be a hole in the course, but no one used it anymore because the water had changed and it was too hard to get to. The poor goose laid there with its head down and almost looked dead.

The Big Guy wanted to leave it alone, but I had to check it out to see if it was okay. I felt so bad for the poor thing. I had no clue what I would do if the thing really did need help, but I wanted to try. I didn't know if maybe it had some string or something wrapped around it. Of course, it was fine. It was just playing dead to protect a nest full of eggs. We got chased by an angry goose that day.

Another time I was following the Big Guy down a path that was supposed to lead to another one of his good fishing spots. I was watching where I was stepping because the ground was very uneven. I was also trying to keep up to him. As I was looking at the ground, I saw something that made me scream very loudly. The Big Guy had stepped on this huge snake he didn't notice. As I got to it, the thing was angry for being walked on and reared up. It looked at me with evil beady eyes and stuck its tongue out at me.

Did I forget to mention my fear of snakes? Well, I don't like them very much and I avoid them at all costs. After I screamed, the Big Guy stopped dead in his tracks and spun around as quickly as he could to see what the matter was. Now our accounting of this is different.

According to him it was a little garter snake that was scared to death of me after I screamed. To me, it was an anaconda and wanted to squeeze the life outa me. To make matters worse was, the grass was really long and who knew just how many of those things were really there!

I was so afraid and shaken by the time he got back to me I didn't know what to do. He tried to calm me down and reassure me I was okay and the poor little thing was gone. I knew in my heart that huge mongo thing was still lurking around waiting to grab me at any second. I insisted the thing was mean because in fact it had stuck its tongue out right at me and tried to bite my shoe.

He got me to continue on down the path promising me of a safer place to fish. After we got near the crick, we ran into an old guy we both knew. After greeting him, he couldn't hardly wait to ask what the heck was that blood curling scream he heard minutes ago all about. He must have thought the whole thing was funny too as he couldn't quit laughing about it as the Big Guy told him what happened.

Personally, I didn't see it that way and found no humor in the story what so ever. I had just hoped that monster of a snake didn't come back. My heart couldn't have taken the shock and I don't think the Big Guy could have laughed any more anyway.

I was always making him do things he didn't want to do when it came to animals. One day we were riding in the country. He tried to avoid a squirrel that was in the road, but he just nicked it. He thought he killed it and since the poor thing was still lying in the middle of the road, I made him turn around to see if it was dead and to move it off the road so it wouldn't get squished any more. I could tell he didn't want to, but after a look from me, he turned the truck around and went back.

Sure enough, the poor thing was still lying in the middle of the road. He called back to me, "I think it's dead!" He moved it with his toe and what happened next was sure surprising. The poor little thing must have been dazed because as soon as the Big Guy's foot touched it, the squirrel woke up and climbed the closest thing there was. This just happened to be the Big Guy's leg! Was the Big Guy ever surprised! He froze right where he was.

That squirrel could have torn him up pretty good, but it didn't. It just sat there on the Big Guy's knee just looking up at him with a "Oh crap" look on his face. The Big Guy said it was like a Zen moment that felt like 10 minutes or more. After a second or two, the squirrel jumped off the Big Guy's leg, ran across the road and up a tree.

He walked slowly back to the truck looking at where the squirrel went up the tree. I was really quiet because I didn't know if he'd be mad or not. The Big Guy just turned to me and said, "I think the little guy is going to be alright." He just turned the truck around and continued on. I know I heard him swear under his breath, but I can't be sure. He found out that day about my soft spot for animals.

I had more patience with animals than I had with anything else. People made me mad and businesses like banks made me madder. I hated dealing with them all in general. The last straw with my old bank came a few weeks before our wedding. We were short a few hundred dollars to pay the band we wanted to hire. We knew we couldn't earn the money before the wedding there wasn't enough time left.

I remembered my CDs I still had in that bank. I suggested we borrow against that and pay it back when the CD comes due. I could tell the Big Guy didn't want to use my money, but he gave in. We went to our bank to see if they would loan us the money. Our banker just couldn't understand why we didn't go to the bank that held the CD's. We both tried to explain our past troubles. Both of us knew they wouldn't loan us the money no matter how much the CDs were worth. Our banker told us to go try one more time and if they wouldn't loan us the money then he would.

We went back to the bank and asked to talk to a loan officer. One of the upper officers was the only one not busy, so he was the one who talked to us. As we walked into his office, I knew he wasn't going to loan us the money. We explained to him why we needed the cash and how we wanted to pay it back. I gave him the paper with the worth of the CD on it. He took a few minutes to look over the paper.

When he finally looked up, he stared straight at the Big Guy. I'll never forget his words. He said, "I don't want to see you spend her money. Go home and think about this and if you really need it, I'll loan it to you." He barely looked at me. I was so angry, madder than the last time.

We walked out of that bank, and straight to our bank and told our banker what had happened. We walked out of the bank with the money we needed. I was really happy. I felt I had everything covered and taken care of. As much as I didn't know what I was doing, I knew I would be doing it with the Big Guy and everything would be okay.

The Big Guy and I talked for hours about our upcoming life together. We talked about what we wanted and what we expected. Every subject we could think about, we put everything right out on the table. He didn't have too many requirements, just as long as I loved him and would be by his side, he was okay with whatever I wanted. I thought that was pretty easy because he was very easy to love and to be with. I wanted to be sure he knew what was getting into when he said the big "I do."

The main reason why we got along so well I think was because we had so much in common. We liked the pretty much the same things. Our favorite color was the same, pretty much our favorite food was the same and we liked to do the same things. Our interests were the same. When we talked about events, we pretty much agreed on the outcome and how we felt about it.

Our hobbies were similar except his was a little more physical than mine. We had the same ideas about what we wanted in life. I couldn't get over how easy we agreed on things. We hardly argued about anything. If we did have a disagreement, it wasn't long before we were making up, and boy, did we love to make up! Even today, he will try to pick a fight just so we can make up. Many times, we skip over the fight and head straight to the making up part. It's the way we were then and it's the way we are now.

We would both rather tear our own eyeballs out of our head with spoons rather than hurt each other, even in play. We love to wrestle and tease one another. I remember once, I got him good. He tries hard to top it, but he can't.

It was when we were dating and he was living in his apartment at the golf course. I was there with him and had to use his bathroom. I was pretty shy about things back then, so I was really careful about expressing such things. I was in his bathroom and realized he was almost out of toilet paper. I had no choice but to use what he had left. An evil idea came to mind, so I thought what the heck.

I flushed the toilet and washed my hands, only I didn't dry them. I walked straight up to him; put my wet hands on both sides of his face and I said, "Do you know you're out of toilet paper?" He had this look on his face, like, "No!!! tell me you didn't!" I couldn't contain myself. I about died laughing. He started laughing too and promised he'd get even with me. I remember it ending in one of the many tickling sessions we seemed to have.

We were constantly doing things to make each other laugh or to tease each other. Every now and then, he will touch my face with wet hands and tell me we are out of toilet paper. I just tsk at him and tell him that was so twenty-five years ago! He just can't seem to get even for that one.

The Big Guy knew all about my life and how I grew up. He knew how hard I had things and he knew how I was treated. He didn't like any of it. He always told me he wanted to make my life better. I believe he has. I also wanted him to know how I felt.

I was sure to tell him I didn't like drinking or smoking. I didn't mind an occasional social drink, but I would not ever put up with him coming home drunk every night or every weekend. I didn't want to tell him what to do because he had liked to drink in the past; I just wanted him to know what things were with me.

I would definitely not put up with him hitting me or any of our children out of meanness or anger. If he wanted to drink, it would be okay; I just wanted him to know I wouldn't be around to watch it. I knew what my mother went through in dealing with her alcoholic husband and by God, I was not going to go through that ever. The Big Guy seemed to understand what I meant and made his choice.

We had an understanding between the two of us. We got to be so close during those times. I'd like to think we still are. I always wanted people to quit looking at who they thought the Big Guy was and see who he really was inside. I wanted them to see what I saw. A lot of people in town didn't like the Big Guy for various reasons. Either they owed him money they wouldn't pay or he had beat them up or someone they knew in a bar fight he used to regularly be involved in. Apparently, the Big Guy wasn't such a nice guy when he had been drinking.

We were up against a lot when it came to the Big Guy's reputation. The Big Guy used to be very angry and had a lot of bad things happen to him to make him that way. He never really had anyone care about him except his mom and he wasn't treated very good by others. It wasn't until he beat up that bully that day in grade school that he started to get people's respect.

After the Big Guy went into the service things changed for him. He learned things in the Army that is not taught in school. Things I'm not supposed to talk about. Let's just say when he came home, he came home a changed man.

He was planning on making a lifetime career out of the Army. Until he fell during a training process that is. The fall wasn't his fault, but he fell just the same. He fell off a rope the height of a telephone pole. He was hurt pretty bad and the doctors didn't think he would ever walk again. Something about the toughness of an Army Ranger didn't make that true.

After a few days and the promise of a date with a pretty nurse, the Big Guy walked out of that hospital on canes. It was a little while after that, the army sent him home on a medical discharge. They said he was just tearing up his knees worse and gave him a choice of either a desk job or coming home.

The Big Guy decided to come home. He told me he tried the desk job, but it drove him nuts. If he couldn't be with his guys, then he wanted to go home. I think it angered him to know that the Army wasn't going to be paying him for his injuries. He didn't get any because it happened during peacetime. If it had happened during a war or if it happened overseas, then he'd be getting pay. It just wasn't fair.

After he came back, he pretty much took up where he left off. He ended by leaving his girlfriend he was supposed to marry because she wasn't exactly true to him while he was gone. He was so disgusted with women; he didn't want a thing to do with any of them. Oh, he'd have his fun with them, but that was about it. He didn't want anything serious or lasting. That was at least until he met me.

His friends were happy he was home and would throw party after party for him. For a time, he'd be in the bar drinking running up a tab until it was so high, they wouldn't charge to him anymore. He'd do some job somewhere, pay off his tab, and start all over again.

One kind of drink really had a bad effect on the Big Guy. Any type of yellow whiskey did it. If he drank that stuff, it made him mean and ornery. He always knew when there was a fight brewing when his friend would set him up with shots of the stuff. When he drank that all someone had to do was bump into him to get him riled. Yea, he was quite the drinker. He told me he was drinking so bad and was so sick he thought he was dying. He figured he gave himself alcohol poisoning.

When he was recovering, he said he took a good

look at himself and asked himself what the heck was he doing to himself. He was pretty down and feeling like a failure with everything that had happened. He had enough mind though to recognize what he was doing to himself was bad so he stopped. That was a couple of months before he met me.

No one would take the time to get to know the Big Guy like I did. I knew he was a good man just from the look in his eyes. He would tell me about things he did and places he saw. Even as a young boy, he was not as bad as what people thought. I always knew there was more to him and I really wish people would take the time to see what I saw. So many people said I shouldn't be with him let along marrying him. I wouldn't listen to them then and I won't listen to them now.

Folks still talk bad about him today. We know this and it angers me. I know it makes the Big Guy angry too, but he won't give in to it. When he is asked or if he hears someone had said something bad about him, he just says if they are talking about me, then they are leaving some other poor sap alone!

This would also make the Big Guy laugh at some of the things that are said. He knows if only half of them were true, it would make him superman. It is even sad when you think about it to know that some people don't have anything better to do than to worry about what is going on in our lives like that. They sure must have boring lives. The way they embellish on things is enough to knock your socks off at times.

The Big Guy is pretty easy to get along with. He only has a few rules you can't break in front of him. He doesn't put up with no one hitting a girl. That really riles him. You don't mess with his flag or his family. He protects me and his children with a vengeance. Sometimes he is over protective in my book, but that's okay. I can't change him even if I tried; even if I wanted to, which I don't.

Even under pressure, his strength shines through. The closer and closer it got to the wedding day, the more I needed him. I depended on him probably more than I should have. Being with him made everything worthwhile. All the fights, arguments, heated moments would be all worthwhile as long as he was my husband.

I wasn't sure if I would be a good wife, but I sure dang was going to try. The more people said we wouldn't last, the more I wanted to prove them wrong. I didn't care what anyone said. When I looked into his eyes, I was looking into his heart and I knew we would last.

The loud-mouthed fella that was supposed to be the Big Guy's friend even had no confidence in us. He bet the Big Guy our marriage wouldn't last three years. He was so confident; he bet $1,000.00 cash money on it. We had a witness that even seen the handshake. That man owes us $1,000.00 but he has yet to pay us, even after all these years.

The night before we were married actually didn't go as bad as I feared. All of the wedding party was together and actually getting along. No one said anything out of line and did what they were instructed to do. We all even made jokes and laughed a lot making things much more fun.

As we practiced what we were to do the following day, I kept thinking, wow, we actually made it. It was hard to believe all the hard work was finally almost over. Everything we did lead to the next day and it got here quicker than I had expected.

The rehearsal supper was held in mom's garage. I know it don't sound like anything special, but any other idea we had was vetoed down. We were told it would either be too expensive or just plain not right. I didn't know where else we could have a dinner of that size and still have room for everyone.

We were getting pretty frustrated in not being able to find a place suitable for what mom wanted when she just said, "Why don't we make the food and just have it here at my house?" She said we can set up tables in the garage and have it outside. It wouldn't matter if it was bad weather because there would be plenty of room in the garage.

So, to please her, we agreed it would be held at her house. The Big Guy and I worked and made sure her garage was clean and neat. We set up tables and decorated as best as we could. I thought it looked pretty nice after all. The Big Guy helped cook and the food turned out pretty good. I was happy with the way it turned out and very glad it was almost over. Like I said, almost.

We did have the cops there that night. Since we had some of the preparations at his mom's house, someone had to drive them over. We all took trip after trip to get the job done. I tried to do a lot to keep others from getting mad that I wasn't doing enough.

With the many trips, I started to take a short cut through a museum yard. There was a road that many people used even though the lady who ran it didn't like it being used. It was considered a city street so there really was nothing she could do to stop it. But she tried.

She called the cops and complained that I was driving through her property way too fast. I wasn't driving any faster than normal but you couldn't explain that to her. The cops were called and they were at my house checking on the complaint. The Big Guy seen them pull up and was the first to go to talk to them. Since he was friends with them, he smoothed the whole thing over, not telling my mom what the problem was. He knew she would have my backside if she knew what was going on. He told her they were just friends stopping by to talk to him. I was so relieved because my mom never found out the truth. It was one less thing I had to worry about.

I guess it helps to have friends in places like that. The cop who was the Big Guy's friend laughed about it the complaint because he knew who made it. This was the same guy who stood in the hall with the Big Guy that fateful day at school when he tried to ask me out and I ran away. Funny how things come back isn't it?

The Big Guy just said she was trying to make trouble and he should go back and just shoot the old battle-ax. They got a big laugh out of it and he just put it down, as the lady was a complainer and liked to turn people in for nothing as she had done in the past.

It just seems to me that things were falling into place no matter who tried to mess things up. I prayed that tomorrow would go off without a hitch.

Chapter 12

The wedding day was finally here. I couldn't believe it as I got up out of bed that last morning. I remember thinking, the next time I go to bed; I will be a married woman. Unbelievable. I started to think of all the things I had yet to do. My family was all home for the event. Not that there was a lot, but they were there. My sister and her husband were home. My aunt was there and my uncle was supposed to be there later. I really didn't care who showed up as long as the wedding took place.

The day was beautiful. I couldn't ask for a better day. There was no uncomfortable heat at all. The day was warm, but not too hot and not too cool. The sky was a beautiful blue with a small hint of clouds. The sun was shining, but not so bright where it hurt your eyes. There was a cool breeze but it was very light. You could feel it, but it wasn't strong enough to blow hair out of place. It looked like everything was going to turn out great.

I remember getting up and helping my aunt in the kitchen, butter some buns to make ham sandwiches for the dinner. She was working all by herself, so I asked if I could help. She smiled and said I didn't have to because I had to get ready. I told her

I had plenty of time and I wanted to help. We made small talk while we worked. There were not many left to do anyway. I had worked the night before and she was doing what was left.

After that, I told her I was going to take my bath. I normally took a shower, but I wanted some time to soak and think. It was still early and there was plenty of time. I didn't get to relax for long because mom was soon banging on the door telling me to hurry. She said there were others who needed to use the bathroom too.

I heard my aunt tell her to lighten up because I had just gone in there. I could tell mom was still not yet accepting the whole thing and was aggravated by her answer. She said she didn't care, that it was my wedding and I should be seeing to everything to make sure things are done.

My aunt replied with, "Things are done and she needs to relax a while." I'm not sure what else was said, because I didn't listen anymore and was not going to waste any time being upset. It was too late for that.

I wanted to look beautiful. I knew I wasn't, but for that one day, I wanted to be so pretty, I turned every head. I knew my dress was me and as pretty as I ever seen despite the price. There was no humidity in the air, so I hoped my hair would cooperate. As luck would have it, I wasn't breaking out. As prepared as I was for any rouge zit with a ton of makeup, I was lucky I didn't need it. Looking too made up wouldn't do either because of the Big Guy's feelings on makeup. I knew I would use a little to help in places where I needed it.

I was a little worried about the dress fitting as I was expecting. It was good it was my first as I was not quite yet showing. At that one time, I was glad I wasn't really a huge girl. If I were, there probably wouldn't be any way I could hide my condition. I didn't really tell anyone and I tried to dress normally.

I did wear baggier t-shirts, but that was about it. I really hoped I wasn't big enough to make the dress not fit. I was busy putting everything I needed together excited about the whole day. I didn't want to let anyone or anything spoil the day. I wasn't going to let it happen no matter what.

Mom didn't say too much to me unless it was to holler, hurry up or to ask what are you doing. Even though she was like that, I tried hard not to let it bother me. I kept thinking I was going to be a married lady today. I was going to be a wife. I had to say it over and over to get used to it because I tried not to think of it before then to keep me from feeling too nervous. I was starting to feel nervous. Not because I was afraid, we wouldn't go through with it, but because I didn't want anyone to say or do something to ruin the memory, I wanted to carry with me from that day on.

I wore a simple t-shirt and shorts to the church. This was so I didn't want to have too many things to worry about. I had my bag full of makeup brushes and combs. I had a curling iron and hairspray. My sister was going to help me with my hair and makeup so she told me not to worry. I had my hair permed a few months before so it still had plenty of curl without looking too stiff. Things were falling into place and everything was going fine.

As we pulled up, I saw the Big Guy with his

groom's men as I ran for the church. I didn't want him to see me and hex the whole "not seeing the bride before walking down the aisle" thing. Us girls were supposed to dress in the basement and the guys were supposed to stay up in the church. We had everything planned and practiced. So far so good.

Everyone was smiling and laughing. I'm really not sure if mom was the whole time, but after I put my dress on and had my hair done, even she said how pretty I looked. Thank God the dress fit me great. I must not have gained that much weight.

While my sister was fixing my hair, the door opened and in walked one of the Big Guy's friends who was standing up for him. He was a guy that had been friends with the Big Guy all through school. He was very embarrassed as one of my bridesmaids had her top off and was in the midst of putting on her dress.

He stopped for a moment looking at me and then he backed up apologizing profusely and closed the door behind him. We all laughed and I was relieved it wasn't the Big Guy. I didn't put it past him to try to get an early peek. I really didn't want him to see me until I was walking down the aisle. He was not going to ruin it this close to the time.

For all the fussing of wanting to see my dress, I wanted it to take his breath away. I wanted him to see me for the first time and lose his mind. That image needed to be imprinted on his mind forever. If he had an image like that, maybe it would last until way past the time when I was old and ugly. I know I was hoping for a lot, but it was my wedding. It was my dream.

My mother did show up for my wedding. After all

those arguments and fights, after all those threats of not going to my wedding, she was there. I was so relieved. I thought she looked pretty in her dress. There were two people who didn't show up. It hurt, but it didn't surprise me.

Mom's boyfriend was one and my sister's husband was the other who didn't go to my wedding. My sister gave me the excuse that he wasn't feeling well enough to stand in church for the ceremony. I never knew why mom's boyfriend didn't show. I never asked him. I figured if I asked, it would just give it more power. I put it out of my mind and concentrated on the day.

Mom walked me down the aisle and gave me away to the Big Guy. It was what I wanted. I know that's a father's job, but mom was the only real parent I had. I figured she deserved it. Anyway, she did it and I was happy. When we stood at the end of the aisle getting ready for that walk, I looked to the end to where the Big Guy was standing.

He had a huge smile on his face. His eyes never left me. I remember thinking I did it. My looks in that dress did it. The way he looked at me I knew. I knew I wasn't wrong in picking that dress. Everything was beautiful. Everything lined up. It was all I prayed for, it was all I expected, it was all I hoped for.

I couldn't believe my eyes. I looked at the Big Guy standing at the alter waiting for me. He was the most handsome man I ever saw. He looked so good standing there in his tux. It didn't matter to me what he was wearing. He could have been buck naked like he threatened, or wearing his speed-do like he said and it wouldn't have phased me.

When I looked into his eyes, I saw a very loving man who could see no one but me. I saw into his heart and I saw what he was promising. I was so happy and I felt so lucky. As far as I was concerned, I was the luckiest girl in the whole world! I could see the love pouring out of him that day. I knew that he promised me a whole lifetime of hugs and kisses.

I knew no matter what he'd always be there by my side to help me, to hold me, laugh with me and cry with me. That was the time when I knew all his promises he made before were true. I knew what we had would last and survive throughout the years to come. My mother was wrong. If she couldn't see it that day, I didn't figure she ever would.

The ceremony went off without a hitch. The only flaw if you can count it as one was when the priest asked for the Big Guy's left hand for me to put his ring on, he stuck out his right hand instead. The priest saw it right off and actually slapped his hand down and whispered, "Your other left hand."

We all giggled as he sheepishly put up his left hand. I remember thinking, oh well; at least he still said I do right. It didn't matter to me which finger I put that ring on because we were married. The kiss was better than I imagined. It was our first kiss as man and wife. I promised myself I wouldn't cry and I didn't until I saw my mother crying. Then my waterworks started flowing.

The priest was pretty good about everything even though he knew my mother didn't approve of the wedding. We all tried hard to leave the church in the right condition. He stressed we were not to get any rice inside the church. He didn't want to deal with the mess. Things went pretty well until we went back in to sign the marriage certificate.

When the Big Guy bent over to sign his name, a whole bunch of rice fell out of his ruffle on his tux. I saw it and was afraid the priest saw it too, but I don't think he did because he didn't say anything. I tried to brush it off the table before the priest saw it. I got caught on camera because the lady we hired to take pictures captured it. I was so embarrassed, but I do laugh about it now.

After the ceremony, we decided to go to a nearby park to take some outdoor pictures. We had already taken a lot of pictures in the church. I always loved to be outside and I wanted some of our pictures to be outside. They turned out pretty well, with the green of the leaves and grass against my white dress. We had our favorite one blown up and it still hangs on my wall today. The huge tree that was there that day is now gone. It's pretty funny to know our love has out lasted such a tree.

This picture has gotten us into trouble with our second daughter. I know I'm jumping ahead a mite, but this deserves to be telling. When our second daughter was around 4 years of age, she could talk pretty good. One day after looking at our wedding pictures, she was pretty riled.

The Big Guy wanted to know what was wrong. She blurted out, "Why wasn't I in your married pictures? I bet you made me stay with a babysitter! I wanted to wear a pretty dress and be in your picture too!" There was no amount of talking or explaining that would help her understand she just wasn't born yet.

She was so angry, she wouldn't listen. It took a while before she would even calm down. We tease her still today about it. She was recently married herself and the Big Guy fondly teases her every now and then that he got to be in her married pictures.

Everyone who was there commented on how pretty the wedding turned out. Even my sister who was at her best friend's wedding a few weeks before said my wedding was the most beautiful wedding she ever attended. She said she liked how simple things were. There was nothing flashy or gaudy. It was to the point and there was no nonsense. It was all comments like I wanted to hear.

At the reception, the food was good and everyone seemed to enjoy it. We took some pretty good pictures cutting the cake. I didn't smash the cake in his face like folks thought I would. I wanted to be nice. I loved him so. I didn't want to mess him up looking as handsome as he did. Just looking at him melted my heart all over again.

Since I was expecting, I only drank one glass of champagne to celebrate the day. Even if I wasn't pregnant, I still don't think I would have drank much at all. I wasn't much of a drinker anyway and I didn't want any alcohol to cloud any of my memories. I watched the Big Guy drink some with his friends. I didn't protest because I wanted him to have a good time and I didn't want to be a nagging wife already. For what I could tell, everyone had a good time.

As he held me during our dance, he looked at me so loving and told me again how happy he was. He said he loved me more and more every day. It was like I was floating with him holding me so close. I think others could see the love because every time we turned around someone was clinking their glass to make us stand and kiss.

I really didn't mind how many times they did that. I'd have done it myself if I thought it would have worked. Anything to be able to kiss him like that. Even with everyone watching I didn't care. He was finally my husband and I was his wife. No one could change that now! His favorite Uncle had even come up to say he thought he married a pretty lady and he was very proud of him! It meant so much to the Big Guy to hear that.

Later I heard about the Big Guy's friend accidentally walking in on us in the basement that day. He said his friend was looking for the bathroom and went the wrong way. He said he was embarrassed about seeing my friend in the nude, but when he saw me, he said, "Your girl is the most beautiful bride I have ever seen!"

The Big Guy told me he wanted to come down to see for himself, but he knew I wouldn't be happy with him if he did that. He told me that waiting to see me walk down the aisle was one of the hardest things he had to wait for. He wanted to see me in my dress now!

The Big Guy said when I stepped out to where he could see me, his heart had melted and the most beautiful woman was standing there in that white dress. As she walked down the aisle and got closer, she even got more beautiful. His buddy reached around the Big Guy's brother who was his best man, and slugged him in the shoulder and gave him a thumbs up and said, "See I told you she was beautiful!"

The Big Guy's brother only stood there and said, "UFF!" The Big Guy said the funniest feeling came over him. It was of love for me and he couldn't believe I was actually marrying him. He felt like we needed to rush the ceremony before someone came and stole me from him. He couldn't believe I wanted him. He asked himself, "Was she not right in the head to marry an oaf like me?"

He said he was so mesmerized by my beauty he didn't know what he was doing when he put the wrong hand up for the ring. All he knew was this beautiful woman was marrying him and he couldn't believe it!

In talking about what happened showed two sides of a coin. We were both amazed at the other. I thought he was so handsome in his tux and he thought I was beautiful in my dress. Neither one of us could imagine what the other seen nor was this actually going to take place. We both felt the same way. We should get this done before either one of us came to our senses and woke up from the dream.

I guess maybe that's why we get along so well. We feel the same and put the other in before ourselves in our wants or our thoughts. He will go without to be sure I have what I need and I will do the same. We are not afraid to make sacrifices for each other. Personally, I think we were a match made in heaven. I just wish my mom and others could see that. I was prepared to try to educate the whole world if I had to. There would be nothing to stop us now.

Chapter 13

After the wedding dinner, he took me to the house where we had planned to live for a while and changed out of our wedding clothes. I couldn't believe we were married and it was safe for us to be together. I kept thinking, "I am late, I need to go home." We picked up our bags we had packed so we could leave to go on our honeymoon. I wanted to say goodbye to mom, so we stopped over at her house. There were a few things I needed to pick up from there as well.

Mom was sitting in her chair in the living room when I got there. She didn't even get up to give me a hug. I packed up what I needed and told her I'd be back for anything else I had left. I told her we were planning a short trip up north and I'd call her when we got back. I could tell she was crying, but I didn't say anything. She sounded so cold and far away, I was glad to leave. I told her I loved her and gave her a kiss and a hug and the Big Guy and I were on our way.

We drove most of the night to get as far away as we could. We both were so tired. We stopped at a motel that had a lot of pine trees around it about halfway to where we had planned to go. It wasn't a fancy place and the room was small, but neither one of us cared. We were both so tired and just happy to be together at last.

Things happened that should have happened and I will leave it at that. It had been a wonderful day followed by an even better night. We held each other all night long with no fear of me having to leave to go home. I teased him about me having to go home or else I'd get grounded again. We laughed and fell asleep in each other's arms and wondering if it was all a dream or not.

After we woke up the next morning we decided to get back on the road. We had a great breakfast and spent some time just being together. It was so nice not worrying if someone was looking over our shoulder and telling me it was time; I should be home. The drive was nice and not hurried. We would have liked to stay a few days in that motel, but our finances wouldn't allow it. I only had the weekend off of work, so we needed to do what we had planned and get back home again.

We really didn't do anything expensive or fancy. There was an attraction we both wanted to see that didn't cost a lot, so we planned to go there. It was near the town where my sister lived, so it worked out. She said we could stay with her during the night and then we'd have our days free to do what we wanted and what our money allowed us to do.

We had a lot of fun even though we couldn't spend a lot. I didn't care. The company more than made up for what we couldn't do. We had some money, but we wanted to be sure we spent it wisely and didn't waste it. I remember the trip home came too soon. I didn't really want to go back, but I was afraid I'd lose my job if I didn't show for work. We had no choice.

On the way home, we stopped at a store that sold a lot of different items. Every time you stopped there would be something different so you never knew what you were going to find. I guess the guy bought things on sale and in auctions, so it made for an interesting stop each time.

When we got there, the items were packed in the place so much, it was hard to walk around. The guy's organizational skills were something to be desired. I guess it made it more like a scavenger hunt, so it was kind of fun. We started talking to the guy and he congratulated us on our new marriage. The Big Guy had found something he thought we both would really love.

Remember I told you about our time spent on the lake in his brother's canoe? The Big Guy found a brand new one that we could actually afford. He was in the midst of haggling for a price when the guy decided to give him a break because it was our honeymoon. The Big Guy said, "I know we could pay bills, but then the money would be gone. This was our wedding money and not meant for paying bills anyway. It is meant to buy something we would enjoy and get some use of." I agreed this was right, so we bought that canoe.

Many the times when money got tight, we thought about selling the canoe. Many people were actually willing to buy it. Neither the Big Guy nor I ever had the heart to sell it. That canoe still sits outside in the yard just waiting for us to use it again. I can remember all the times we took it to the lake and had a blast with it. Through the years, because of many reasons, we stopped using it.

The kids grew and we grew and it seemed to be too small. Other times, we just didn't have time to strap it on the top of the car. One day we will take it back to the lake again, but for now it sits there waiting. Every time I look at it a memory comes back and I smile. I'm not sure we will ever sell it.

The trip home was slow and depressing. I had morning sickness and didn't feel well at all. As much as I wanted to be with the Big Guy, I just wanted to lie in something that was not moving. It wasn't meant to be because I had to get back to work that next day.

Turned out, I didn't make it to work after all because I was so sick. I almost got into trouble over that one because I had still not told anyone I was expecting. I was going to get wrote up at work for missing until I explained that point. They said they understood and gave me an oral warning instead of a written warning. I guess this was better but it didn't matter at the time. It was a low paying go nowhere job I needed to try to pay bills, but I was not happy with it at all.

Married life seemed to agree with me. For the most part, I felt great. I really didn't have morning sickness all that much, just a couple of times really. I considered myself lucky because I had heard most expectant mothers got it and it was horrible. When I got it, I knew I was getting it, I got sick and I felt better. I was glad for that because I sure didn't like to get sick.

If we were not at work, we were in bed. Seems like most of our waking hours after we got home were spent lying next to each other. It felt so good to be by him, I never wanted to get up. It was like pulling teeth to get up and go to work. I had spent so much time having to go home and be away from him, now all I wanted to do was to be close to him.

I would tease him at night after I got home from work about having to go home and he was making me late. He would laugh and say, "Don't be teasing me little girl, your grounded! You are home and you're staying home. You're not going nowhere! I want to control you!" He'd tell me this to make fun of what my mom used to always tell me. She always wanted to control me. It would end up in a tickle session and we'd always laugh about it.

It seemed like we were joined at the hip. We watched TV together, we ate together and we would just sit there and be quiet together. We had talked so much; we didn't feel a need to have to talk. It was so comfortable to be together. I was happy, he was happy. All that was needed was for us to find a way to earn our way. We didn't have a lot of money and we knew we were not on an easy road. The new baby would need things and we would need things to take care of him or her. Yes, our lives were still changing.

The house we lived in belonged at first to his sister. It was located right next to his mom and dad's house. His sister and her family decided it was best they moved out and got a new place to live in the next town. Because the house would be up for sale, his older brother decided he would buy it to finally have his own house. He was generous enough to agree to let us stay there while it was in the process of being remodeled. Our money was not enough to afford rent someplace else, so we agreed. The Big Guy would help him with the work on the place for our rent. For the most part, it was a pretty good trade deal.

Since we did live there, we took on the bills of the place. We paid the heat bill, electricity, water, phone, and cable bill. We also had our car payment so we were pretty strapped. Our money just never went far enough. I don't know how we would have made it through those first months if it weren't for his family. The house was pretty much torn out because everything seemed to need to be replaced. The Big Guy's sister and her husband couldn't really afford to do any upgrades or repairs so it was in pretty bad condition.

The first winter we were together we lived out of three rooms. The upstairs had three bedrooms and a bathroom and the downstairs was completely gutted out. We had to use his mom's kitchen when we wanted to cook and she let us use her shower in the basement.

For some unknown reason to me, his brother felt he had to tear out the bathroom as well. It would have been fine, but he didn't put it back for months. Do you know how hard it is to be pregnant with no close bathroom? It was really no problem during the day to go next door to use their bathroom, but who wanted to get up out of a warm bed to go that far to relieve yourself. So, I punted and kept a bucket close. It worked out so I'm not really complaining, just explaining how we lived back then.

The house was cold that winter. A new furnace was put in, but the insulation was some time in coming, so it was cold. I remember not having our own refrigerator and storing our milk in the window downstairs because it was cool down there. I would get up to frozen milk most mornings.

At least it didn't spoil so that was a good thing. When it was cold like that, we just put more blankets on the bed and cuddled closer. It didn't bother me at all. It really didn't matter if we lived in a cardboard box because we were together. That is what mattered the most.

The Big Guy was constantly checking on me to see if I was warm enough. He was always covering me up to be sure I didn't get cold. I didn't mind this attention at all and always snuggled in closer to him. He made me feel very good and I loved it. I would tell him, "Yes, I am cold." just so he would pull me in closer to him. He was always so much warmer than I was anyway. I always called him my brick.

Even today I snuggle up close to him. He says through the years he has leaned to sleep white knuckled on 2 inches of bed. If it weren't for the sheet he was desperately holding on to, he'd end up by sleeping on the floor. If that happened, I know I'd be down there right next to him because I can't stand to sleep without him anyway.

One night after work his sister was there to pick me up instead of the Big Guy. I had no clue why and all she would say was he has a surprise for you! For the life of me I could not figure out what it was. When I walked into our door, I hollered for him right away and he answered, "I'm in here" from the bedroom. There he was laying on the bed with a little kitten no bigger than the palm of his hand. After a bunch of ooo's and ahhh's, I instantly asked him, "What about your no cat in the house rule?"

Before we got married, the Big Guy laid down one rule to me. I would be allowed to have any pet I wanted; I just couldn't have any cats. Especially in his house because he told me he hated cats. Under no circumstances was I to ever bring a cat home. I didn't say too much when he told me because he knew how I was. I told him long before about my soft spot for animals and I also proved it. Here he was sitting on our bed with a kitten he brought home. I was so surprised. I kidded him and called him a big softy.

He had to tell me of how he brought that little thing home. He was at a farmer's house when he noticed the huge number of cats the man had. He commented on how his wife would love to have one of those kittens. The farmer said, "She would? Well, she can have her pick!" Just then, the Big Guy noticed this scared hungry little kitten sitting off by itself and said, "I'll take that one."

The little thing seemed happy to be picked up and took right to the Big Guy. He put the poor thing in the seat of his dad's old Chevy pickup truck he was driving and started for home. It wasn't too far down the road when he looked over to see the kitten and to his surprise, the thing wasn't there. He pulled the truck over along the road to look for it. That's when he noticed the big holes in the floor of that old truck.

Just thinking he might have hurt that kitten made him feel terrible. He figured it was probably lying dead on the highway. He turned the truck right around and drove really slow just looking along the road for the kitten. Of course, he didn't find it.

He felt like too much like a heel to go back to the farmer to ask for another kitten, so he just turned around and headed home. He said he felt so down about the whole thing. He parked the truck and was going to go in to talk to his mom when something on the floor caught his eye. When he got down to look under the seat, there was that little kitten curled up in a ball sleeping. Was he ever relieved! He took the little thing in the house to feed it and to wait for me to get off of work.

His actions kind of tells you of the Big Guy's heart, don't it? If he were that cruel and mean, he wouldn't have thought of me enough to bring the kitten home. When he couldn't find it, he could have just continued on home without a thought of the poor little critter, but no, he drove all the way back to that farm just looking for it. I knew I had a man with a good heart and that day just proved it. Getting a new kitten out of the deal was a good thing too, so I felt like I was getting the better end of the stick.

That cat was a very good cat. He never made a mess and he just loved attention. He waited in the window like a dog for me to come home and then it was in my lap time. Funny thing was, he wasn't my cat after all. That German Sheppard puppy we had took to that cat like he was her baby. She watched over that cat and wouldn't let anyone hurt it. They would play for hours.

We would have to separate them at night because if we didn't, all you would hear was something little run down the steps then something big would follow. Something big would run back up the steps then something little would again be following. The thumping up and down the steps was enough to drive you nuts but it really wasn't that bad until the cat decided to come in our bedroom and run under the bed to get away. The pup would try to get under the bed after it and make the whole bed shake and that's what usually woke us up. Enough was enough especially at 3 am! We'd have to lock one or the other in our room just to have any peace and quiet at all.

I remember the dog chasing other cats out of the yard just to protect our cat if there were any cat fights. She'd always come back and sniff our cat as if to say, "You alright buddy? I gave that other dang cat what for!"

One day a fella stopped by to talk to the Big Guy. The cat had walked up and rubbed up against his leg. The fella bent down and was playing and roughing up the cat a bit when the Sheppard got in his face and growled softly and showed her teeth. The man froze in his tracks and asked, "Does she bite?" The Big Guy says, "I don't know, but that's her cat and she don't like you messing with it." The guy laughed and said, "Nice dog, I'll leave your cat alone." and he backed up. The dog just sat there staring at him as if to say, "You best not be hurting my buddy!" It was pretty funny to see them being friends like that. I still have pictures of them sitting together in our armchair. It sure was a sight!

As the months passed, I got bigger. Not too huge, but bigger to me. I know now looking back at the pictures, I could have hidden my condition pretty well, but at the time I felt like a whale. My body had changed so much it scared me. The Big Guy kept telling me I was beautiful and was very happy the titty fairy came. I don't know what he was looking at, but all I saw was a fat gal with huge sore breasts. I was depressed because nothing fit right and I could not get comfortable no matter what I did.

I didn't know what to expect. I would feel this movement in my belly that would amaze me. I would always grab the Big Guy's hand so he could feel it too. During the night when the baby was more active, I would put my belly against his back so he could feel the kicking like I could. He would tell me to quit kicking him and I'd laugh and say, "Wasn't me, take it up with your child!"

It was all a new experience. I know I was probably ornery at times, but that was to be expected. The Big Guy loved me so much, he didn't care. We just did the best we could and waited for the new baby to show up. We tried one day to go to one of those birthing classes because I was getting nervous about the birth. Even I said we don't need those because of the silly things they tried to make us do. The doctor had explained things well enough and that was fine with me. I had just hoped the pain wouldn't be too bad and the baby would be healthy.

I was doing everything I thought I should to have a healthy baby. I was trying to eat the right things and the Big Guy and I still went on walks real regular. The cravings I had were kind of weird. The over whelming hunger I felt for anything that was related to beef was strange to me. All I knew was I wanted it and now. I had no patience to wait.

The Big Guy would try his best to see I had what I wanted which was Slim Jim's and beef jerky. I would get a hankering for it and bug the Big Guy to go to the store to get me some. Back then, I would have killed for a steak. I was sure this baby was going to be a linebacker for all the meat I was eating and all the kicking it was doing. I had hoped it would be because the Big Guy really wanted a son. For me, as long as the baby was healthy, that's all I cared.

As the day the baby was due came closer, my doctor wanted to see me more and more. I didn't think I needed all that checking, but after all, he was the doctor, he should know. I was still working and had planned to work right up to the day I had the baby.

The Big Guy and I even went to Social Services to sign up for help for the 6 weeks I was planning on taking off work. We drove over there many times to fill out paperwork. We tried to get as much help as we could because we knew we needed it. I wasn't sure we would qualify, but it was worth the try.

Since my work knew I was expecting, they pretty much let me take off when I had my doctor appointments. It wasn't a problem as long as I told them about each appointment as soon as I knew about it, which I always did.

On these days, I would go in early and leave about a half hour before the appointment and come right back to work after I was done. I would stay late to make up for the time I missed. They were fine with that because I always got my work done and so was I because I couldn't afford to miss anytime at all. It seemed to all work out.

My doctor had wanted to see me once a month, then changed to once a week the closer my due date was. After that as the day was getting closer, he wanted to see me even more because he wanted to monitor me.

I remember it was a Monday and I was supposed to see him again. I went into work at 6 am and left at 9 am. I was back at work by 11 am and worked until 6 pm. The doctor had said everything was on track and he'd see me in few days. The Big Guy had been going with me to all my appointments and had told him not unless we see you first.

The Big Guy told the doctor he thought I was going to be going into labor soon, but the doctor didn't agree. He said since it was my first baby, it was going to be really hard to tell and he didn't think I was ready yet. I remember laughing about it wishing it would be over soon because I was getting really uncomfortable with my growing belly.

That night after I got home, I was so tired. Getting up extra early and going all day really tuckered me out. I went right over to the Big Guy's mom's house because I knew he would have my supper waiting for me. He always did whenever I worked late like that. I was glad for it because I was hungry and I was tired.

We spent almost an hour at his mom's house before we decided to back over to our own house to watch TV before going to bed. I was very glad to be able to relax on my couch that night. All I wanted to do was to sit there, relax and put my feet up. Our German Sheppard climbed up on the couch and was sitting with me when it first happened.

I had a clock we had gotten for a wedding present sitting right on top of the TV, so I knew what time it was when the first contraction hit. It was 7 pm on the nose. I had other contractions days before, but that's all it was. A sharp pain that was there and then went away. I didn't think a thing about this one because it felt like the others.

I was sitting there holding the dog when the second one hit. It was 7:05 pm on the nose. I remember thinking, wow, I don't think that is right, but I didn't want to get excited about it just yet. I had heard stories on how women in their first deliveries had false labor. They felt pain and went through the motions to go to the hospital just to find out it wasn't time and go back home again.

I didn't want to start ringing bells only to have it be false labor. I was too tired for that. All I really wanted was to sleep. So, I said nothing and continued to watch TV.

The third one hit right at 7:10 pm. Now I was getting concerned this was more than just a pain. I remember thinking, "Okay calm down, wait until 7:15. If one hits then, say something." So, again I waited for time to pass.

Yep, 7:15 hit with another one only much harder this time. My dog was looking at me like, "What was that? I think I might have squeezed her a little hard with that last one. The Big Guy was sitting in the chair relaxing and watching TV. I casually asked him, "Honey how would you like to have a baby?" He says, "I know honey, we are having a baby." I say, "No, I mean tonight, now." He says, "But I'm tired you don't want to have this baby tonight, I'll miss Mickey Mouse's Christmas that is coming on TV!"

I told him I didn't care what was on TV, I just had four contractions and they were already 5 minutes apart! He finally took me serious hearing that. I knew he was kidding, but I was not in a kidding mood just then.

He called the doctor and he was told not to bring me in until the contractions hit 3 minutes apart. The contractions were coming pretty regular, so I knew it was getting closer to be time to go. I told the Big Guy, I wanted him to walk me over to the bathroom because I had to go NOW!

I was afraid of what might happen when I was alone and really wanted to hold his hand. He just laughed at me and said, "Okay, honey, I'm coming to help you." The walk took a while because I was feeling so weird. I was afraid to walk fast and with a contraction to hit at any time, I didn't want to be in mid step.

I remember being on the toilet hearing his mom tell him she didn't think it was real that I would probably be home again later if he took me in to the hospital now. She thought because this was my first, I didn't know what to expect and was getting excited over something that would pass.

As I took care of my business, I noticed I had passed blood. I now knew it was the real thing and not false labor. I was really scared and just wanted it over. If this part hurt this bad, I was afraid of what was to come. How bad would that hurt and how long would I be sore for?

His parents let us use their car to get me to the hospital. Our car was broken down and we'd been trying to get it fixed. Some yahoo had put pop in our gas tank when it sat in the parking lot of where I worked. Other cars had been vandalized along with it, but we were having a time with our insurance company. They just didn't want to pay for the repairs.

It was not a time to be without a vehicle.

I even sat on a plastic bag in case my water broke. I didn't want to make a mess on the seat of their car. I called my mom to let her know I was going to the hospital. She was so excited. She had so many questions I didn't want to answer mostly because I didn't know. I just told her I didn't know how much time it would take and yes, she could go to the hospital whenever she wanted. She had asked if she could be there before and I guess she must have forgotten my answer with all her excitement.

After all, this was her first grandchild and she had never seen a baby being born before. I wasn't sure I really wanted her there, but I didn't want to take away the experience for her, so I agreed to let her watch if she felt she wanted to.

We got there in plenty of time. We had preregistered, so that process went pretty fast. The contractions were coming a lot closer and a lot harder. I felt every bump in the road on the way over and walking was pretty much out of the question even though I knew I had to. I couldn't believe how much it really hurt. I didn't really yell or anything like that, just worked hard at breathing through them like I was supposed to.

The Big Guy was so sweet being by my side through the whole thing. I remember the terrible pain coming and going just as quick as it came. I couldn't believe it, but I actually slept between contractions. I was so tired. I didn't think I'd be able to do this. I was really scared. The Big Guy looked like he was more scared than I was. He kept looking at me with those big blue eyes of his. Those wonderful blue eyes seemed to say, "I love you honey, are you alright?"

I remember thinking how sweet he was looking at me like that. I really appreciated him being there and I tried to say it. I remember looking at his eyes and putting my hand up to his cheek to tell him how much I loved him.

The next thing I knew a contraction had hit hard. When it was over, and I opened my eyes, he was there pulling something out of my hand and the nurse was asking him if he was okay. I asked him what the heck he was doing?! He just said, "I'm cleaning my beard out of your hand."

Here when I put my hand to his cheek, I pulled out quite a handful of his beard when that contraction hit. I didn't even feel when I clenched my fist and pulled my hand back down to my side. I felt so bad knowing what I had done! I could only imagine how much I hurt him. He said he felt like half a bull dog with his cheek lying in his lap. The nurse said she didn't have to normally have to doctor the dad's during labor but in this case, it was the exception.

From that time on when I was pregnant, the Big Guy would never take me to the hospital ever again before he shaved his beard off. If we met up with any couple who was expecting a baby, he'd take the guy aside and tell him to be sure to shave that beard off or he'd regret it. He would tell about his experience with me. He said it hurt so bad, he couldn't believe it.

It was even years before beard would grow back normally again. I believe it was like 12 or 13 years before it filled in again in that spot, but who was counting. He still cries about it today if you ask him. He says a man should have a full growth of hair if he wants to grow a beard. If you look really close today, there still is a little spot that won't grow any hair. I tell him to look at all those razors I saved him from. I don't think he saw the humor in that at all.

That night seemed to be longer than it was. The pain was really bad and I was so tired. I think I took it pretty well though, because there was only one time, I screamed the whole night. After I got there, it seemed like it was forever until they took me into the delivery room. Forever in all reality wasn't that long because I got to the hospital by 9 pm and I gave birth at 11:00 pm on the nose.

My mom was there and she was beside herself. They let her watch through a little window as I was in the delivery room and she had her hands full of handkerchiefs and was biting on her nails. Every now and then I know the doctor would look at her with a thumbs up to let her know everything was going as well as it could.

Because I was so small the doctor had to cut me to keep me from ripping when the baby was being born. That happens when the baby's head is still too big to fit through and the soft tissue tears. The doctor cuts just before it rips to have a clean cut that will heal easier.

I'm sorry for being so graphic for all you gals who has not given birth, but that was how it happened. You all should know what you are getting into before you decide to take that step with your men because it can and will happen to you. No getting round it.

Anyway, the doctor had made the decision to cut

me. He told me about it as he was giving me a shot to numb me so I wouldn't feel it. I must have been in enough pain because I didn't even feel the needle poking into me. What I did feel was when he cut in a place where he didn't get quite numb enough.

That is when I screamed as he cut, the doctor quickly apologized that it was his fault. If I wasn't in the predicament I was in, I probably would have slapped him for it, but it was too late by then. The cut was made and the baby's head was coming out.

My whole labor and delivery took 4 hours. I was really surprised that was all the time it took. When it was happening, it seemed like days because 4 minutes of labor pains is way too much let alone 4 hours. I've heard tell of other ladies taking way more time than that, so I wasn't too upset with it. Even the doctor was surprised because he said I sure went fast. With it being my first delivery, he expected it to take longer. He had just gotten there to check on me when the nurses told him I was ready to deliver.

See, the nurses are the ones who are there with you while you're in labor. There is really nothing much for the doctor to do at that time anyway. You are in pain as your body goes through natural contractions to widen the birth canal to allow the baby to fit as it is being born. Until this is wide enough, you have to lay there and take it because the baby won't come if it can't fit. This can take hours or days depending on the person. All you can do is wait it out and take it the best you can.

Let me tell you, a woman loses all thoughts of modesty when she gives birth. They strip you of your clothes and you are in so much pain it seems like anyone walking through that door is going to stick their arm up places it doesn't belong to check out how you're doing. After a while, you just feel like you don't care what happens and all you want is for it to be is over. That's all there is to it.

Chapter 14

After she was born and yes, I said she, I was so relieved. She was a beautiful petite baby girl. I couldn't believe I had given birth to a new little life. The Big Guy was so proud; he didn't seem to care about his beard at all.

My mother was flying. All she could say was, "Thank you so much for my new little granddaughter!" She even told me that when she drove down town to buy a present, she left her lights on in her car. Some guy told her, "Hey lady, your lights are on!" and she just smiled at him and said, "I don't care, I'm a grandma now!" That guy must have thought she lost her mind because all he did was laugh at her.

As tired as I was, I just wanted to sit and hold my new baby. We took turns that night sitting holding her and counting toes and fingers. She was so perfect. I couldn't have asked for a better baby. A person just can't explain the feelings when you you're your new born baby. I guess every new mother feels the same way. You want to hold her and protect her forever and never let anyone hurt her.

I knew then it was meant to be and she was our little gift. I loved the look in the Big Guy's eyes as he held her and talked to her. I knew he was going to be a great daddy. I just hoped I would be a good mommy; Lord knows I had my doubts.

When it was time for me to go home from the hospital, I knew I couldn't bring our baby home yet. Our house was in the process of being dry walled and the dust was everywhere. There was no way I wanted to bring my new baby home to that mess. It would be a couple of weeks before the work would be done and the mess could be cleaned up.

My mom was the one who suggested I bring the baby home to her house and stay a while. I was afraid to do this as I didn't want to deal with what she would throw up to me later. I knew I had to put the baby's needs ahead of my own in this case.

I would have to brave the consequences in order to keep my baby safe and healthy. So, when I was discharged from the hospital, I went home to stay with my mom for a couple of weeks.

It worked out pretty good at first. Mom was really good with her new grandchild and I loved to sit and watch Grandma hold the baby. She was so proud of the baby and it seemed like I had finally done something to make her proud of me.

The Big Guy didn't like me being there either, but he also knew the baby needed a clean home to live in. All he could do was work harder to get the house cleaned up so we could come home. He spent as much time between coats of plaster and sanding with us as he could. I knew we would both be happier when we could come home again. I was still afraid of what might happen.

One afternoon when it was close to the time the Big Guy was supposed to come to see us, he was late. I didn't worry because I knew he had probably just gotten side tracked again. It happened and it was usually never a problem because I trusted him. He had decided to go to the grocery store to bring me some food and milk when it happened. By the time he got back to me, he had a story to tell.

He asked, "Did you know we broke up?" I said, "No, that is news to me? What are you talking about?" He laughed about the whole thing. He said the checkout lady at the store was quite sympathetic about it. She said she heard we broke up and she was sorry to hear it. She thought we were a cute couple and would stay together for a long time. Was there any way we would ever get back together again?

The Big Guy just smiled at her and said, "No, she won't quit her drinking and running around." He turned and walked right out of there without saying another word. He said he wanted to let her think it was true. If she wanted to believe gossip, then he'd let her. He thought it was quite funny but I didn't see any humor in that what so ever.

Talk about the rumors that fly from a little dry wall dust. I couldn't believe what someone had made up. If you knew me at all, you knew I didn't drink, ever. I never ran around and if I did it was because I was chasing the Big Guy because he was all I ever wanted.

You sure got to love these small towns and their love for gossip. I guess if it floats their boat, it's okay, I just worry about the people that get hurt by it. I wasn't afraid of getting hurt, but there are others who don't have the strong love the Big Guy and I share.

I stayed at mom's house for a little over two weeks before I was able to go home. She was mad when I left because I didn't stay longer. She said if I did stay for the month, she could claim me for fuel assistance and get more money.

What she didn't realize is if I didn't go home when I did, then we couldn't get credit for me and the baby and we wouldn't be able to get fuel assistance. We still had to pay for heat for the house and our heating bills alone were over 400.00 a month.

I was barely making that where I worked and we had other bills we had to pay. I don't know how she expected we would make it at that rate. Never the less I went home and she was mad at me again.

Things seemed to get better for a while after that. The baby was new, our life was new and my mom's appreciation for me was new. I was so afraid of hurting that new little baby. So much had changed and I'm not sure I was ready for it. I guess it didn't matter because the baby needed me to be better. I sure grew up fast let me tell you. So much I had to do and be responsible for. I tried hard not to mess things up.

The baby was so little and needed care. I had to get into a routine with her. Bath time in the morning and the round the clock feedings took up most of my day. Changing diapers was not too bad and I seemed to have a ton of clothes for her that people had given me. I was afraid of doing things wrong and making her sick. She seemed to be doing well because the doctor was very happy with her checkups.

The Big Guy was a very good daddy. He didn't mind the baby wasn't a boy. She was his little girl. He was so proud of her. He spent hours holding her just singing to her and talking to her. Telling her she was the most beautiful baby ever and he was always going to be there to protect her.

It was something to see. I was afraid to walk that path, but I knew I would be okay because I wasn't doing it alone. As hard as things would be, we would be okay because we were facing it together like we were meant to be.

After a few weeks it seemed like I was getting the mother thing down pretty good. I was tired a lot, but the baby was healthy and happy. It was money was what I started to worry about. I wasn't working and the Big Guy was having a hard time finding a steady job. We were trying, but without my meager paycheck, we were sliding in the depths of debt even faster.

Social services were no help either. They kept making us go back and fill out more paperwork just to tell us they needed to check things over. We were driving our car on empty because we had no money for gas. The baby needed to be checked on, so we had to make many trips to the doctor fearing we wouldn't make it back home again. We finally got one check from Social Services for $289.00. It came the week before I was to return to work.

The first day back to work, I marched straight in the office to ask for a raise. I hadn't had one and knew I was a good worker. I had reports back from my co-workers that they really missed me or more missed the work I got accomplished. I did special projects that nobody else took the time to figure out how they were done and after I was gone and the boss asked for them, they were told I did it and I was gone. They agreed to my request and gave me a 10-cent raise. I know that's hardly anything, but at the time it was a little something, so I was happy.

I did however have to report the raise to social services. They in return sent me a letter saying I was now making too much money and no longer eligible for their help. There was that making too much money thing again. And like before, I didn't understand how that could be. We were not making it. Bills were mounting up and there was never any money for groceries or gas. I guess that is their definition of making too much money.

I went back to work and the Big Guy continued to look for a job while taking care of our baby. He was a regular mister mom. He did a really good job and I can't complain at all. I tried to do what I could when I got home, but I was still tired from having the baby. I am not sure if I was depressed or not, but I know our money troubles weighed heavy on my mind.

When we brought the baby home for good, we didn't have a real crib yet. We were trying to get one, but it hadn't worked out. I knew we'd have one in a week or so because I was taking the money out of my check to pay for it. I felt bad we didn't have one soon enough but we did the best we could. I wasn't sure what to do or where to put the baby so she would be safe as she slept. The Big Guy did though as he was pretty good at figuring out how to get by with what we had.

Our furniture wasn't much, but we did have a

cheap Chester drawer. He just took most of the clothes out of a deep drawer leaving some in for padding and fixing it so there was nothing hard to rub on the baby. She was always wrapped up in a soft blanket anyway, so that didn't matter. He just put her right there in the drawer. She was light enough and it was sturdy enough, so there was no fear of it tipping. I was amazed at how he could come up with these things. I don't think I would have thought of that by myself.

Our baby was doing fine. She was growing and gaining weight like the doctor wanted. I had been breast feeding which is something I chose to do. I had wanted to breast feed her for several reasons. First off, it was way cheaper. We didn't have much money to buy formula and it helped out for the first 6 weeks. I had researched the whole thing and found out it was way healthier for the baby anyway.

Besides the fact it was easier at night. I didn't have to listen to a screaming baby while the bottle warmed. I'd do a quick diaper change and then go lie back down in bed with her as she ate. I did fear falling asleep with her in the bed. I was so afraid of hurting her and rolling over on her as I slept. I just never seemed to get enough sleep and while I fed her, I was so comfortable I had a hard time staying awake to put her back in her crib when she was done.

She was eating fine between every 2-3 hours. This worked out when I could stay at home with her, but I knew the time would come when I would have to return to work. This bothered me terrible because I just wanted the best for her. We started talking to others who already were through this stage to see what they did. It was pretty obvious I wasn't the first to deal with this, so I decided it was best to take advantage of experience in the matter.

My sister-in-law told me what she did for her kids and it seemed to have worked for her, so I figured it was worth a try. Her daughter was a preemie and needed special nutrition. I didn't think I had to go to that extreme, but her advice sounded pretty good.

She told me to get some infant cereal; rice would be the best for a new stomach. I was to mix a very small amount in her bottle she had before I put her down for the night. The cereal was to give the formula some body. The problem with babies is they mainly eat, sleep and mess their drawers.

Their awake time is pretty minimal and the reason they wake up is either because of wet drawers or an empty tummy. She said if you fill it good before they go to sleep at night it stands to reason it will last longer so they sleep longer. All I can tell you is I tried it and it worked!

I knew in order for me to be able to work all day, I would have to get sleep at night. I don't know what is with this, but mothers seem to acquire a better sense of hearing when it comes to babies crying at night. I swear the Big Guy could sleep through a neutron bomb most nights. Not that I minded getting up, it's just I was really tired and I just plain didn't have the energy.

After giving the baby this special bottle, she slept longer at night, which was heaven for me. I started doing this a few days before I had to go to work. I had to wean her off the breast milk and on to formula because I wouldn't be home to feed her anyway.

I was amazed at how much nicer it was to have the baby sleep most of the night versus waking up every 3 hours around the clock. She seemed to thrive and was actually more alert during the day which suited me just fine. My doctor on the other hand did not agree, at first.

I say at first because when he asked what was I feeding her and dumb old me told the truth, I got chewed out like you wouldn't believe. I felt like I was back in school in the principal's office being yelled at like that. I almost asked if there would be a detention later, but I thought better of it considering the doctor's anger.

I just let him spout off about how I was damaging my poor baby's tummy. Didn't I know that a baby could not handle any solid food until they were at least 6 months old? Did I realize the unfix-able damage I was doing to her? Apparently, I didn't know, because I was feeding her, she was liking it and she was healthy, happy and sleeping most of the night away.

When I got the time to get a word in, I just told him as calmly and politely as I could to stuff it. I told him if he wanted to feed my child every 3 hours, he was more than welcome to come to my house and do it. I would leave the door open and told him not to wake me because I had to go back to work, which meant I needed to sleep at night. I told him I don't know about his job, but mine don't allow for naps during the day.

He wasn't too happy with me but did comment on how healthy she was and how her weight gain was great. He told me I could do what I thought was right because the baby didn't seem to be showing any signs of mistreatment and I agreed. I was the mother after all.

It was about 6 months later when that doctor apologized to me for what he said. He was newly married like I was and his wife was expecting their first child. When he yelled at me, he was quoting facts from a baby book from college. He found out with his own experience with his own baby that those books didn't cover everything.

Through his own experience, he found out that each child was different which meant each had different needs. He now realized that if a baby was hungry, you feed it. As long as the food agrees with the baby and does not create a bad reaction, it should be fine. He apologized and told me I was right and he was wrong.

He also thanked me for the tip because now he could sleep all night through because his baby was sleeping more as well. I should have written that on a calendar. That sure didn't happen too many times!

As our baby grew, so did our knowledge. We are not unlike every other new parent. Trial and error are not bad things. I learned new things and ways of doing things every day. It was amazing how this little new person could teach an old dog such new things. The cat learned new things too. He learned not to walk so close to the play pen when the baby was awake.

The baby was older, but not quite walking yet. The Big Guy had her in the playpen, which had bars on it. It was low down close to the floor like a normal play pen was. He was busy in the kitchen and left the baby to play in the pen with her toys. The cat walked quiet like and passed the pen.

Normally he didn't get to close to the baby, not because he didn't like her, but because I tried to keep him away. I was afraid she would pull his fur and he would scratch her, so I didn't allow it as much as I could. Boy did that cat learn his lesson.

The Big Guy heard this ungodly screeching coming from the living room. He could not imagine what it could be as he ran to find out. It sounded like some poor creature was dying a horrible death.

He almost died laughing when he saw what was going on. The cat like I said had walked right past the play pen. Quick as can be, my wonderful innocent daughter reached through the bars and grabbed his tail. She had both feet planted on two bars and was trying to pull that cat in the playpen with her backwards.

She had a pretty good grip on his tail and was not letting go until that cat made it through the bars. Of course, that cat was too big to fit, hence the screeching and clawing at the floor. He was trying to find some kind, any kind of traction to pull him free of whatever that was that had his tail!

It was a pretty funny sight let me tell you. The Big Guy was laughing so hard while he was trying to get the baby to let go. He wasn't doing a very good job of it because her little hands held tight. All he could hear was that poor cat screeching and my sweet baby laughing so evil he couldn't believe it. He finally got her to let go of the tail. The cat ran for the hills and the baby was still giggling.

The Big Guy said he went to find the cat to be sure the poor thing was okay and he swore the poor cat had indents on his backside from the bars that would never go away! The cat was fine and it turned out okay.

We were both amazed at what a good old cat he was. He could have turned and clawed and scratched her to make her let go, but he didn't. The only time in fact when he did finally scratch her was one day when he was eating. She walked up behind him quiet and tried to sit on him. She startled him and he turned and got her with a claw. It wasn't very deep and I figured she had it coming that time. I sure miss that cat.

We lost him shortly after that. He got sick and hid from us. By the time I found him, it was too late. We had taken him to a vet to see if we could save him, but he was too far gone. He had dehydrated and was too weak to make it. Apparently, he had gotten a hold of some poison the neighbors put out for the squirrels and chipmunks they considered pests.

I don't know if he got the poison direct or ate a poisoned animal. All I know is we lost one of the best cats we ever had. Everyone mourned especially our Sheppard. I felt so bad, but there was nothing I could do.

We loved having a baby and did our best not to spoil her. It was inevitable though because she was mom's first grandchild, our first baby and the newest baby in while for the Big Guy's side of the family. She was so sweet and cute it was hard not to make a fuss over her.

I wanted to buy all the cool toys I never had as a

kid, but of course, because of our lack of funds, I couldn't spend that kind of money. I would pick out what I thought was the neatest toy and save for that. The family did go over board at buying her stuff, so she did have many toys she probably didn't need.

She had clothes like you wouldn't believe. People were giving me such cute outfits for her, there was no way she could wear them before she out grew them. I was so proud of her and the way she looked in the pretty clothes. I loved to dress her like a little doll. I was very happy with the way things were turning out. My thoughts would return to school and wonder when and if I would be able to go back.

I did apply for school the following year. The Big Guy was hoping he'd find a steady job to help out with our money problems. That didn't happen, so I had to continue working my measly paying job. It was better than no job at all and I couldn't hope to find a better one with no college degree or experience. It was a hopeless circle. A person needed a good job. You couldn't be even considered for the job unless you had a degree.

Experience was also needed and if you didn't have that, you probably wouldn't be hired. How could you ever get experience unless you got hired? I didn't have the answer to that question either. So, I stayed at my job hoping I could climb a ladder there and make more money. Unfortunately, I could not no matter how hard I tried. I was definitely stuck in a rut.

After I applied to school, I got the letter saying I was accepted to attend again. I felt pretty good about this as they still only accepted 40 students a year. I had time to make arrangements and fill out for financial aid. No matter what I did or how hard I tried to work things out, I could not see how we would survive as a family if I quit working full time.

I knew I could not work full time and go to school full time. There just were not enough hours in a day for that. The payments we had to make would not be made on a part time income. The Big Guy felt terrible because he still had not been able to find full time work. It just was not working out.

I could not sleep. I worried about how we were going to make it constantly. I tried different scenarios, and nothing would work out in my mind. One of us would have to work full time to pay our bills. It was pointing to me being that person. It hurt so bad to realize my dream of going on to college was dying. I didn't know what to do. I knew mom would again be so upset with me. I knew I was again letting her down.

The Big Guy did everything he could to make money. When he could not find work, he tried to make work. Everyone knew him and his older brother were pretty good small engine mechanics, so he took in every lawnmower he could to make money. He even bought junk mowers to rebuild to make good ones to sell. It wasn't great money, but it helped. The bad thing was, it wasn't steady money. We needed steady money to survive.

I remember one day my sister-in-law and her daughter was visiting us. I was in my kitchen washing my dishes and just chatting with the Big Guy's sister. All of a sudden, her daughter burst in my house hollering for me to come quick! She said the Big Guy was killing his brother and she wanted me to stop it!

I dropped what I was doing and ran outside.

Sure enough, the Big Guy was sitting on top of his younger brother as he was lying on the ground. One hand was around his throat choking him off and the other was beating him in the face. I could tell by the Big Guy's red face; he was very angry and had pretty much lost it. I ran down to him as quick as I could. After grabbing the Big Guy and pulling on him backwards, he moved and finally let his brother stand up. I quickly got in between the two and pushed them apart as far as I could.

His brother hollered at me asking me what the heck was I doing and I was to get out of the way. I hollered right back, "I'm saving your dumb backside!" and immediately turned to the Big Guy. I put both my hands on his shoulders and talked to him to get him to look at me. I kept saying, "Whatever he did to make you mad, it isn't worth it to kill him. Your mom will be so angry with you. Don't do it! Calm down! I love you; it will be okay."

After I finally got him to see me, he started to calm down. He was so angry and I was so afraid he'd do something dumb. Not that I was afraid he'd hurt me, but because I was afraid, he'd hurt someone else and they'd take him away from me. I have only seen him like this a few times and I have been the only one who could calm him down. I just fear for the time if I'm not there. The poor other guy that made him mad would pay dearly.

When I found out what made the Big Guy so angry, I wanted to beat the tar out of his brother too. I couldn't, not because I wasn't physically able to, but I knew violence didn't solve anything. I sure wanted to I can tell you that much.

The Big Guy had a used rider that he had fixed up to sell. It was a pretty nice one and he knew he could sell it for a lot of money. Money we desperately needed. A few days before the Big Guy was very happy because he was finally able to sell that mower. The customer had given him half the money down which was $400.00.

That was a fortune for us and the promise of another $400.00 meant we could pay some bills and have money left over to either save or buy something we really needed. Life was good and we were happy.

That was until the customer got there and the Big Guy went down to the shop to get that rider. It seems that his brother decided he would borrow it the day before without asking the Big Guy. He had mowed yards for folks for money and had a yard to do. This yard was pretty rough and had a deep ditch in it. Instead of mowing it by hand like he should have, his brother wanted to use a rider so he didn't have to use a push mower and walk it.

When he went over that ditch, he broke up our rider pretty good. He could barely push it home it was so broken up. All I know was when our customer got there and saw the condition of the new mower he had just bought, he was not happy.

Of course, the Big Guy had to give him his down payment back. We had to scrape the $400.00 back up to repay the man to keep from losing a good customer. There was no way the Big Guy could even fix the mower as the deck was demolished beyond repair. This is why the Big Guy had lost it, seen red and was beating the tar out of his little brother. It wouldn't have been so bad if his brother had paid what we lost, but he didn't. He wouldn't man up and pay for what he had broken. We were just out.

The Big Guy's mom was pretty angry at him for hurting his brother like that. She wouldn't listen to any explanations and took his little brother's side. Even his older brother said he was a jerk for beating him like that over a dumb rider. The Big Guy could not win with his family. He was a dirty dog no matter what.

It was about a week or so later the Big Guy had to pull his older brother off of his little brother. I guess that yard needed to be mowed again but this time he decided to use his older brother's brand-new John Deere mower. This mower was a lot more expensive than the Big Guy's mower he had ruined earlier.

His older brother did not take it too well when his expensive mower was the one that was ruined. The Big Guy was laughing when he pulled the older brother back. He told him, "Now it's a terrible thing to beat your little brother like that over a dumb old mower!" His older brother was so angry cussing and saying how stupid it was to break such an expensive mower on a yard like that. I guess what goes around comes around don't it.

Like everything else, we did survive those times. We worked hard and tried to do what we thought was right. Because I couldn't go back to school like I wanted, our plans for the future didn't stop. Some things just got put on hold for a while. It hurt me to realize school wasn't going to happen, but I kept telling myself that I was young and I had the rest of my life to make that dream happen.

The Big Guy even made another promise to me. He promised that when it was right and our kids were older, he would pay for me to go to school. I knew it would happen. The Big Guy never made a promise he didn't keep. I would have to work hard and wait until the time was right.

I hated to tell mom about my decision. The thoughts of saying to her, "Mom, you were right, I'm not going back to school any time soon," really was not on the top of my list. She was already pretty critical of my mothering skills. I didn't need that added in on top of everything. I did need to get it over. Another one of my grandma's sayings was "No sense in crying over spilled milk." I guess I've spilled milk before and this was no different. I know Grandma was right, but it didn't make it any easier.

Mom was so angry I didn't think she'd ever forgive me. I hate to tell you the things she said to me. I knew she wasn't going to like it and I was right. I did think I saw a little smile or maybe it was a sneer because I got the feeling, she was happy she was right and I was wrong. I felt that way a lot. It was pretty bad when I made mistakes and was wrong, it made her happy to know she was right. That never set right with me, but I knew it was true.

The Big Guy would often tell me not to worry about my mother. He would say she was a bitter old woman who never really knew true love. She was mad because her marriage failed and mine has not. He felt she was jealous of me because I had what she did not.

I did wonder if this was really true and sometimes, I could actually see it myself. This always made me sad. I felt bad for her that she never truly had what I did. I wasn't talking about money, an expensive car or a nice house to live in. I was talking about knowing true love, giving it and having it returned. Then I would again remember how lucky I was to have a man who truly loved me heart body and soul.

Chapter 15

Winter passed finally and spring was here at last. Things were slowly getting better as we were getting a handle on being parents. I really wanted our own house because living in his brother's house was not the best situation. His brother was fine, but it was his little brother who was driving me nuts.

He never gave us the respect of knowing the house was our home. He walked in at all hours of the day and night to watch our TV and to hang out. It never mattered if we were home, gone away or in bed sleeping. He just let himself in and turned on the TV. He never cared how loud it was or if it woke us up. It really irritated me.

We had spent all winter with our pup training her to be like a well-mannered German Sheppard should be. The pup had her cat to play with, so we were constantly being entertained by the things they would do. After our new baby came into the picture, we had our hands full. It was never dull let me tell you.

We'd go up to his mom's house to be greeted with, "Where's the baby?" or, "Where's the puppy?" Sometimes I think she enjoyed their company over ours, but I didn't complain. The fuss she made every time we took the pup or the baby home got to be so bad, I just told the Big Guy one day, "Honey, give your mother the dog, would you?"

He couldn't believe what I was saying. He asked again, "What?" I said, "Your mother loves that dog and that dog loves her. It just is not right to separate them. Give her the dog and later, we can get another." He smiled at me because he knew what I said was true and he knew how happy it would make his mother.

So, to her house we went again with that dog. We stayed a while just visiting and then we decided it was time to go home. The Big Guy says, "Mom, we'll see you later." and we walked for the door. The dog was lying on the floor and didn't move as we tried to go. His mom says, "Didn't you forget someone?" I replied with, "Nope we didn't, she is yours Grandma!"

She couldn't believe what I had said and had to ask what was that? I told her, "Grandma, that dog loves you and you love her, you can have her." She couldn't believe it and made such a fuss over the dog. I don't think Grandpa was too happy about it, but he didn't say anything. I know he was just trying to be grumpy about it because he loved that dog too. He just didn't want to show it.

From that time on that old lady spoiled the heck out of that dog. She bought the best dog food for it to eat. Every time she went shopping, she'd have to buy a box of Rice Crispies just for that dog because she had to have her bowl of cereal every morning.

When the Big Guy was growing up, he wasn't even allowed to lie on the floor because his mom would say he'd mat the carpeting. That dog got full run of the house; she could go anywhere she wanted.

His mother even went to a very expensive furniture store and bought a love seat just for the dog.

She kept it covered with blankets to protect it from the fur, but if you sat down on it and the dog came up to you and looked at you, you got told to get up off her couch, because the dog wanted to sit down!

It was incredible to see. That dog was a very good dog. She never made a mess and there wasn't a mean bone in her body. She did protect what was hers and she considered the whole family, cat, and all to be her family. I don't regret bring her home and I don't regret giving her to my mother-in-law. I did tease her about being a dog-napping Grandma though! It wasn't the first dog she spoiled on the Big Guy.

He had a coon dog who was very good at hunting. The Big Guy took him to the woods constantly. He was a mix breed of dog. He had some Sheppard with a blue tick hound and maybe a little collie. I am not exactly sure what he was, but he was a big dog who was built with muscle. He was a good dog who loved everyone. The only thing was, he didn't like other dogs.

The Big Guy used to take him everywhere and once when he was out fishing this dog had even saved his life. They were fishing in this little trout stream that was in this farmer's field. The back side of the stream was nothing but bank and cliff and the other side was flat field.

He was fishing and not paying attention to what was around him like he probably should have. The dog was used to wandering around smelling things, so it wasn't a worry where he was. All of a sudden, he heard this snorting and stamping behind him. When he turned around, there was a big mean bull standing there getting ready to charge. The Big Guy looked around to see where he could run to, but there was no where he could go.

He was really getting worried when out of nowhere the dog was there in between him and the bull. The dog would growl at the bull and look back at the Big Guy. He was wondering what that dog was up to when it hit him. He says, "Well don't look at me, take him!"

That's what the dog was waiting for because he lit out after that old bull chasing him clean across the field, barking, growling and nipping at that bull's feet. After he had chased it off, he trotted back to where the Big Guy stood. He petted the dog and thanked him and said, "Good boy, now let's get the heck out of here."

On the way back to the truck, they ran across a skunk and the dog started to do the same thing. The Big Guy hollered at him, "NOOOO, leave that one go boy, let's get to the truck!" He sure didn't want the dog to tangle with that critter!

The dog was a pretty good hunter as well. He wasn't a loud tracker like the other dogs were, he just followed along with the pack and waited until the other dogs got the coon cornered somewhere. Then he'd take over.

He'd go in and fight the coon. The Big Guy once seen him pick up a 40-pound coon and shake him like a rag doll until he broke every bone in that coon's body. He was sure amazed at the dog's skills. He fought other dogs like that too, he just didn't give up and he was tough as nails.

After he brought him home, his parents built a kennel to keep the dog in. When the Big Guy would leave him there, that's when his mom spoiled him. The Big Guy had to work, so he would leave the dog there during the day. She'd come out, feed him, talk to him and baby him. She spoiled him something fierce. After that, the dog seemed to be afraid of his own shadow and wouldn't leave the light of the flashlights when the Big Guy took him hunting again.

He was mad about it, but not that mad because he knew his mom loved dogs and all she did was give the dog a little love. Okay, maybe it was a lot of love! That was the extent of his dogs until he got that Sheppard for me. I think she was always destined to dog nap every dog the Big Guy brought home because that Sheppard of mine sure loved that old lady!

Time flew by and with everything happening, I could not believe my new baby was turning one year old! She grew so much it was incredible. I know having children is not anything special, but I think it is special for each parent to watch a child they made grow and evolve into their own little person. My child was no different.

I believe we all think our own children are more beautiful and smarter than any other kid born. We were no different. I still had to be away every day and work to try to make ends meet. The Big Guy was the one home with our baby. I was glad because he was able to do that, was and is a great daddy.

I got increasingly better at calling the Big Guy, Daddy. As much as it was not in me to call anyone that name, I knew I had to get over it for my baby's sake. Every day he taught me more about what a real daddy was. Sometimes I would be angry because it was at that point when I realized just how much I had missed out on in my life. There is the "don't cry over spilled milk" thing again, but it was hard not to. I tried hard not to feel sorry for myself. I just kept the pain inside and kept going.

It seemed like the months had flown by when I was cleaning the house for my daughter's first birthday party. I remember thinking back at how things were and how much everything had changed in such short time. Mom was still very happy with her granddaughter. She was trying to accept the Big Guy as my husband. I knew it was hard for her, but I thought things were getting a little better.

She's still constantly was at me for things she thought I wasn't doing right or for things she thought I could do better. It's not like we fought as much anymore. I know there were times she would yell; I would listen and take it. Then at night when the Big Guy and I were alone, I'd cry about it to get my feelings out. I knew the Big Guy still couldn't stand to see me cry, but I couldn't help it.

It was the spring after the baby was born and the weather was beautiful. We decided to try to go out to the woods to do some hunting. I asked mom if she'd watch the baby for us while we went. She agreed to but made me promise we'd be back by a certain time because she had someplace, she wanted to go. I promised we would, so off we went.

Up to this point, I had never killed an animal before ever. The Big Guy said he wanted me to try to hit a squirrel because this year during deer season, he wanted me to try to shoot my own deer. I knew I couldn't but I was going to try anyway. He kept talking to me about it and told me to chamber a round when I saw a squirrel. I had been shooting at stumps and pop cans before this.

I saw a squirrel and put a bullet in the chamber, but I didn't fire. I just couldn't bring myself to fire at a poor little defenseless animal. After that I didn't see much to shoot at to burn up that bullet. I happened to notice the time and was afraid we were going to be late, so I told him we had to hurry back to pick up the baby. We double timed it back to the car and started to put the guns away. I had clean forgot about that bullet in my chamber. I checked to be sure the gun was on safety and started to dump the unspent rounds out of it when my finger hit the trigger.

I was in such a hurry, I didn't follow my safety rules and forgot to open the chamber. I shot myself in my hand as my finger accidentally touched that trigger. The safety latch didn't work right on that gun and it flipped off without me noticing it. I remember the surprise at the shot and the instant pain I felt.

My reaction was to grab my hand and bring it close to my belly. The Big Guy was so afraid I shot myself in my belly the way I was holding my hand like that. I relaxed long enough to show him and he quickly took off his shirt to wrap my hand up. He put both rifles away as quick as he could to get me back into town.

The doctor was still in his office when we got there. I told the Big Guy to get over and get our daughter while I was being taken care of or else, we'd be in more trouble with mom. He reluctantly left me to pick her up. The doctor said I was lucky. I missed everything important and just got skin. I didn't hit any bone, tendon or vein.

It left a pretty good mark though and always reminds me to take my time with weapons no matter how late I am. I remember almost passing out after looking at it under the light. The doc told me I best sit down before I fall down. I was relieved to see the Big Guy walk through the door again. He took me home and I remember missing a few days of work from that fiasco.

It wasn't long after that when the Big Guy finally got better job. He had been working for a pizza place before this. It was money, but it had no benefits which we desperately needed. The new job was working on the street crew for the city. You'll never guess who his new boss would be.

If you haven't guessed it, I'll tell you. His new boss was my mom's boyfriend. I don't know if he tried to make things right by giving him a job or if he did it for me or what. He had told the Big Guy to apply because he knew there was an opening and surprisingly enough, the Big Guy got the job.

This was a very good thing and for once, it seemed like things were looking up. I knew the Big Guy really didn't like mom's boyfriend. I knew he would put up with him and bite his tongue for our families' sake. There was not a problem with doing the work; I knew he could handle it. I just didn't know how long the Big Guy would put up with the crap he now had to take. The job was some security for the mounting bills we now had. I knew he had to deal with much more pressure, but I was very glad for the money and benefits. The real worry was the additional stress the job would be putting on him.

The Big Guy was very proud and it was not easy for him to do jobs like he was told to. It wasn't that he wouldn't take orders, but mom's boyfriend was old school and constantly insisted on doing jobs the hard way. The Big Guy wanted to use equipment the city had to make the job easier, but he was continually told to take a shovel and do things by hand.

It really irritated him because he was more than qualified to run the equipment. He did like the freedom of being sent out to work by himself though. He also really enjoyed doing the work and he was actually good at it. He understood how things had to be done and why.

The problem was trying to make Mom's boyfriend understand his skills. One day, the city's grader broke down. It wouldn't start no matter what they did. The Big Guy thought he knew what was wrong and said so. His boss just told him not to touch it that he wasn't going to let a young pup tell an old dog what to do. Besides he didn't think the Big Guy knew a thing about it.

The Big Guy got mad said it was just out of time and needed to be adjusted. He tried to say it wasn't that hard to do. His boss wouldn't let him touch it and told him he was having someone who was an expert drive down from the city to fix it.

This expert charged the city from the time he left his office, his travel time to get there, his time to fix the machine, lunch time and travel time back to the office. When he got there, he told the boss what an easy fix it was because it was only out of time. He showed him to do what the Big Guy had tried to explain. His boss just gave the Big Guy a dirty look as he walked away laughing about it. Yep, some big expensive expert was being paid a higher wage and knew the same thing the Big Guy knew.

It was the little things like that was what the Big Guy couldn't stand. Yet he put up with everything. It was a good thing he got the job and we finally had benefits because a few months after that I had made another new discovery.

The month before during our "quiet" time, the Big Guy had expressed to me what he really wanted to do with me. Now you are not going to hear details because that is still very personal to me. What I will tell you is I gave into him because he was so sure you just didn't get pregnant every time. I'm here to tell you I DO get pregnant every time because the next month something was missing again.

It wasn't that I didn't want more babies, it was just I didn't think we were ready for any more. It was hard enough just trying to provide for the one we had. The Big Guy was happy about it and started making plans about the upcoming new addition. Me, on the other hand, I wasn't so sure.

This time I was so sick I didn't know which end was up. I would feel horrible, get sick and then feel worse. It went on like that for almost a month straight. By the end of it I was really questioning my sanity and wondering why the heck I was doing this again.

It wasn't so bad after I got over the morning sickness. My cravings were about the same as the first time. I knew the Big Guy tried to stock up on the Slim Jim's and beef jerky again. I again had that special glow and our family was happy for us. I knew they worried because they thought like I did. Could we really afford to have another baby? Whether we could afford it or not, it was going to happen no getting out of it now.

I knew mom had mixed feelings about the upcoming birth. I knew she was happy another child was coming, but I think she worried more on if I could handle it or not. She stepped up her nagging and constant reminding me of what I was doing wrong.

I again would just sit, listen, and cry after she was done. It got so bad I was not even allowed to answer the phone anymore. It would ring and if it were her, the Big Guy would not let me talk. He would make some excuse and finally he had to tell her if she couldn't talk to me and couldn't be nice and not make me cry, then she wouldn't be allowed to talk to me at all. He told her I didn't need the stress she was putting me through. She seemed to finally understand and didn't holler at me too much after that.

I thought we were doing okay the way we were. I was still working and the Big Guy was working. The Big Guy's mom was babysitting our daughter, and had already told us she didn't think she could handle a newborn too. We had some decisions to make about how we were going to handle this.

I started to call around to see what baby sitters and day cares charged. I really didn't want some stranger watching my babies, but I knew we couldn't keep asking Grandma to watch them. She was older and had raised her kids. I felt it was unfair for her to have to babysit for us. She would never take any pay when we offered. The Big Guy usually just went out and bought something she wanted for pay because she wouldn't accept cash. I wanted to do the right thing and didn't want to make anyone angry in the process.

The cost of child care was unbelievable. I couldn't get over how much an hour everyone charged for babysitting. When I babysat, I just got a standard dollar an hour. It sure wasn't like that now. I still wasn't making that much money with my job and I discovered I would be working pretty much for 40 hours just to pay a daycare.

If I were to make any money to bring home, I'd have to work overtime every day. I couldn't see that, so it was settled. I would quit my job after the baby was born and stay home to raise my own kids. Besides, we still had our band which was bringing in some extra money.

Grandma agreed to watch the baby until I had my new one so I could at least work and earn as much money as I could. That seemed to make sense, so that's what I did. I gave them my notice to stay in good standing with the factory. They said they were sorry to lose me, but they understood when I explained my reasoning's. I knew I didn't have to explain squat to them, but I wanted them to know that I just was not making enough money to pay a daycare and make it worthwhile to be away from my babies.

Secretly I had hoped they would give me a huge raise to keep me, but they didn't. They just said they understood and would keep me there until I left to have the baby. I remember thinking, boy that is gratitude for you, but realistically, they didn't even have to do that, so I was happy. At least there was an end in sight.

My second pregnancy went pretty well. I was sicker in the first few months than I was from the first one. That was understandable as no two pregnancies ever went the same. We were really hoping for a boy this time because it would satisfy our plans. If I had a boy, I knew he wouldn't ask me to have another child. If it were another girl, I would probably have to try at least one more time because the Big Guy really wanted a son. All in all, I just wanted the baby healthy no matter what sex it was.

There was also another family member expecting and had a baby before I had my second. The Big Guy's little brother was seeing a gal who got in the family way before she should have. It didn't bother me any except I could see so many differences in their relationship compared to ours. I knew theirs wouldn't last a lifetime. The Big Guy tried to tell his little brother to be careful, but it didn't do any good. He didn't listen.

One day he was at our house bragging about the things him and his girlfriend were doing. The Big Guy started to tell him to use protection because he should be careful, he didn't get her pregnant. He just says, "I know she isn't pregnant because she just had her period!" I was amazed at that logic, but it wasn't my life, so I didn't worry too much on it. I had my own troubles.

The very next month, he came to us to tell that she was in trouble and he was the father. Man, do things come back to bite you in the backside or what? We could have told him I told you so and I think we actually did, but it didn't matter because he now had a rocky path to walk down.

The Big Guy's mom was so upset. She was a stout Catholic and those things just were not proper. I knew what the Big Guy and I had done was not proper either, but we took care of it and was married well before our first baby was born. They on the other hand did not do the same.

Personally, I didn't think they should have just for the baby's sake, but that was only my opinion. I didn't think it was right to try to make something work that was doomed from the start. As I watched them together, I saw things that said, "This couple should not be together." I guess it really didn't matter because they didn't listen to anyone.

This gal had her own problems with her family and they ended up by kicking her out of their house. She had no place to go. We really didn't have room for her and since we didn't own the place anyway, we couldn't let her stay with us. The folks had an old camper set up in the driveway. They let her stay there because she had no other place to go.

The folks didn't like it, but they couldn't let her stay in a car, so they had no choice. I let her take a shower and spend time down with me for a while. I thought it might do her some good to have a shoulder to lean on and someone to talk to even though I was warned against it. I was told how strange she was and I should stay away from her because she was nothing but trouble. I didn't listen and befriended her anyway. Boy I should have listened to that warning.

She started to tell me all sorts of things my mother-in-law was saying about me. I heard about everything I was doing wrong. I didn't keep my house clean enough, feed my child the right things and I wasn't home enough. I couldn't believe what I was hearing. It was the first I had ever heard of things like that coming from my in-laws.

I started to think about how mad they must be at me, so I eventually stopped going up to their house to talk. I figured I had a backside chewing coming from them and I wasn't about to let that happen easy. Let them come down and tell me in my own house was what I figured. So, I stayed away.

It was month or so before my sister-in-law came down to talk to me one day when I was home. She was pretty nice about it when she asked if we could talk, so I welcomed her in. She immediately wanted to know why I was so angry at her mom. She wanted to know why I started saying all those bad things about Grandma and why I stopped going up to the house.

I about dropped my teeth I can tell you! I told her first off, I was never angry at Grandma! I never said one bad thing about her, but I sure heard a lot of bad things she was saying about me. I asked when and why she had gotten so angry at me. I told her all I did was try to take care of things the best way I could and work as hard as I could to help pay bills.

She started to get mad, but not at me. She told me of how her brother's girlfriend would sit for hours and tell Grandma all these bad things I had said about her. It really hurt her feelings and she must have thought it was true when I stopped going up to her house.

I told her I thought Grandma and I needed to talk things out and she agreed. I went straight up to Grandma's house and gave her a hug and told her how much I missed her. I started to tell her how I thought she was angry with me and all the bad things I was told she said. She got mad too, but again not at me. We all figured it out right then and there. We were never to take anything this gal said as truth until we find out from the source.

Turned out she wanted to start a new fight between someone, anyone and take some heat off of herself and the predicament she was in. She thought if we were arguing, we would forget about what she was in trouble for. I had news for her. I would not put up with that kind of behavior at all.

After that, I stayed away from her and didn't let her in much to do anything. I was pretty frustrated and ticked off at her. I had enough of my own troubles without her trying to start more for me. I couldn't have that at all.

They had their little girl soon after they finally found a cheap apartment. I had helped them move to be nice. While his brother was working and she was in the hospital, I went over to their apartment to clean and to set stuff up to look more like a home than a room full of boxes.

I knew how she would be feeling after giving birth and unpacking boxes is the last thing you want to do when you get home from a hospital. I put my bad feelings aside and helped them out because deep down I knew how she felt. I had things looking kind of homey when she got home and she seemed happy for it. I didn't get any real thanks, but I didn't mind because I kept it in my head, I'm doing it for the baby.

She wasn't much of a mother in my book. I knew she was new at it and would learn, but I didn't think it should take that long. I had to learn how to be a mother and grow up with my first baby. I figured she would too in time.

It got so bad that even the Big Guy got on her for trying to feed the baby a bottle that had not been warmed. She tried to say the baby didn't like warm milk, but the Big Guy didn't believe it. He just took the bottle away, warmed it up and sat and fed the baby. She drank it just fine and wasn't so fussy. Some people are just thick.

Anyway, I had my own baby to worry about. She was born almost 2 years from the birth of my first baby. 2 years and 10 hours to be exact. I was again cleaning the house because we were going to have the family come over to celebrate our baby's second birthday. I wanted to try to have everything done. I was carrying laundry up and down the stairs all day when I stepped wrong and fell down the last three steps before everyone got there. I had a few bumps and bruises but I was okay I thought.

The family made fun of me falling and said I was lucky I didn't bring on labor pains. I remember laughing and saying I was not due for at least three more weeks. I wanted to have the baby and get it over with, but I wanted to see if this year maybe I would have the New Year's baby since my due date was around then. I didn't think too much more about it the rest of the night. We had a birthday to celebrate.

It was early the next morning when I got the first pain. It woke me out of a sound sleep. I rolled over to let the Big Guy know what was happening. He wakes up and says, "Well at least Mickey Mouse's Christmas isn't on TV this time!" I still don't think he forgave me for making him miss that show!

I just laughed and said I was going to get ready for the hospital because I had that feeling. He said he would take me as soon as he shaved his beard. He reminded me again that I was not going to pull half his face off this time! The pains had started at 5 am. I knew I would have the baby before long. I told him if he was going to shave, he best get it done quick.

I called mom who was already getting ready for her job. She was very excited, but bummed because she had to go to work and she would miss it. I told her not to worry that I would call her as soon as the baby was born. I told her since there was nothing, she could do anyway to help the process, I would let her know when she could finally hold the new baby. I knew it would be a long morning for her because she did love the grand babies.

I knew what to expect this time when I got to the hospital. I knew I would again lose all modesty as every nurse would become very personal with me. I just wanted it over. The pains came and went like before and again, it hurt like the dickens. I breathed through it and did my best not to pull anything else off my husband. I knew I would never live it down a second time.

The only thing that upset me is my normal doctor was not there. They told me who was on call and I got nervous because I had never met him before. I wanted someone I knew to be doing the catching and I wasn't ready to trust someone new.

The new doctor came in to meet me and to assure me he knew what he was doing. I guess I didn't have any choice as I needed someone, so I relented and agreed to let him deliver my baby. The pains were getting harder and more frequent, so it wouldn't have mattered what I wanted, he was delivering that baby today.

The Big Guy was again very sweet and was there for every second of it. He told me he wouldn't have missed seeing his baby born for anything. His boss had let him off for the event, but as soon as the baby was born, he would have to go back to work.

I didn't like this, but at least he was there with me through the important part. I remember pushing and praying, just let my baby be okay and let my baby be a boy. I was getting tired of the pain and sure didn't want to think about doing this a third time. The baby finally popped out at 10:18 am with no complications. The doctor says, "It's a girl!" I looked at the Big Guy standing there holding my hand and all I could say was, "A girl…it's a girl!" I closed my eyes and thanked God for her being okay so far.

I was very tired and very happy. I didn't mind after all she was a girl. She was beautiful and healthy and that is all that mattered. What I didn't like was the fact the Big Guy couldn't stay with me. He had to leave to go back to work. He promised as soon as he was done, he would return. I kissed him good bye and told him he best be quick about it.

I called mom as soon as things calmed down. I remember asking for her when I called the office where she worked. I was told she was in a meeting and couldn't be disturbed. I knew she would want to be disturbed, so I told the lady I was her daughter and I just had her grand baby and I needed to tell her about it.

The lady seemed excited too because she told me to wait and she'd see what she could do. It was only a few minutes when mom's voice was on the phone wanting to know everything. She almost cried when I told her about the birth and the new baby. She promised she'd be there as quick as she could and for me not to worry. I told her to come safe that I and our new baby would be waiting.

She later told me how she was in this meeting when her boss got word, she had a phone call. She walked right out to take the call and was a little afraid when she went back to the meeting. She thought they might be upset with her for leaving like that. She walked back in the room and all eyes were on her. She sat down and waited. She expected to get yelled at, but was surprised when her boss just said, "Well, tell me about your new grand baby!" She wasn't in trouble after all!

Coming home this time from the hospital was a very happy time. I could come home and not to someone else's house. It would have been better if the house was really ours and I could have refinished a room just for the baby, but I was happy just the same. The baby was gorgeous and healthy. The only problem she had was called new borns rash. It almost looked like a bad zit problem, but it soon went away.

I had plenty of baby supplies because my friends from work had gotten together and given me a surprise baby shower. I had all kinds of the newest gizmos and gadgets I could ever want. For the time being, I was happy. I didn't have to work anymore and I could finally stay home and be with my baby like I should be. It was all working out.

The Big Guy was proud as punch over the new baby, but I knew he still wanted a boy. He asked me one day after the birth how I felt about having one more baby. Really, the memory was still fresh in my mind and I certainly was not ready to go through that again. I knew how important it was for him to have a son, so I told him how it was.

I told him there was no way I would consider having another baby until I could bring our baby home to our house. When he bought me a house and I could fix up a room for the nursery any way I wanted, then we would talk about having our third child. Until that happened, he was not to ever mention it to me ever again.

Chapter 16

Our family seemed to thrive with every day. We worked and tried to get along the best we could. Bills came and went; problems came and went and laughs always seemed to be present. The kids were growing up and life was moving along. The Big Guy and I seemed to keep our love and closeness. The kids were normal in their arguments and daily activities. Mom loved being a grandma and seemed to be accepting the Big Guy more and more. There were our occasional disagreements and arguments, but all in all, it wasn't too bad.

I survived going back to school and graduated with honors. It wasn't high honors as I tried for, but it was honors just the same. The Big Guy was proud as punch of me as I accepted my diploma. I knew my work wasn't over because I now had to find a job using my degree, but I was glad the studies were over. It had been more than I wanted, but I wouldn't give up on it.

I had gotten better jobs through the years and the Big Guy had been building his business. We weren't what I'd call well off, but we were okay. Our kids never went without and we always had a roof over our heads and food on the table. We did what we needed to and gave our kids what we could. I'd like to think we gave them a pretty good childhood. I know we have many memories of fun times and laughs. I know some things could have been better, but who does not feel this way.

We never forgot our music or quit playing. After our second child we did have to give up on the whole band thing because of different reasons. Our members seemed to want to go their own way and it was very hard to find musicians who thought the same way we did. Most wanted just to play and make money. They didn't care about making it to practice to have a good sound. We just couldn't play for money and not have a good sound, so we decided to let it go. Our weekends were pretty much booked up with events anyway and there just was not time for both.

The Big Guy and I did still continue to play for our own enjoyment. We didn't care if others liked it or wanted to listen. It was just fun to sit and play with no pressures to make no mistakes. It felt good. Many nights the Big Guy would spend his time playing his guitar while waiting for me to come home from work.

I remember one night he even had to call me at work because he wanted me to hear a song he had just wrote. He was very excited and thought it was pretty good and didn't want to wait for me to get home to hear it. He said he wrote it for me and it was all about our love. I sat at work listening to him sing and play this new song over the phone. I was really touched and thought it was beautiful. I want him to play and often ask him to sing my song because I am so proud of it.

I am very happy with the way my life turned out.

Even though mom thought I had made a big mistake by marrying the Big Guy I knew I had not. I was very happy and knew that just our being together proved it was the right thing. We are one of the few couples that have been married and actually stayed married. Many of our friends are on their second or third marriage or are even messing around and have lovers they shouldn't.

People are amazed when we tell them how long we've been married. To tell the truth, I am amazed because to me it just doesn't seem like all those years have passed. I still feel the same love I felt back then only it is more intense and stronger. Just when I think I can't love the Big Guy any more I seem to love him double the next day.

My children grew up the way I wanted them to. They grew up with knowing there was love in the house. They grew up with seeing their mom and dad hug and kiss each other. The phrase "I love you" was said often and hugs were frequently given. I wouldn't let the kids leave the house without a hug and a kiss. When my kid's friends' folks were either split or fighting and afraid of divorce, my kids were comforted by our love.

Our door seemed to be a revolving door for our children's friends. I never knew how many extra kids would be home when I got there. I even stopped counting heads or asking who are you when I got home. I would just tell them house rules and to wash up for dinner.

I sometimes wouldn't even know which one was sleeping on the couch the next morning when I got up. Our house seemed to be a safe house for those who needed a friendly place to go. I always told all who stayed to be sure their folks knew where they were. I worried about them and wanted to be sure they weren't in trouble. Most all were good kids and we tried to help those we could.

Many of these kids would tell my own kids how lucky they were to have a dad like the Big Guy. They thought he was cool because he would spend time doing things with them. Either talking or playing games or just being a shoulder when they needed someone to listen to them. He was keeping his promise to me in being a dad that could be counted on. Not once did I ever have to put the kids in the car and go down to the bar to bring daddy home like mom said I would have to do. I was never sure if she was happy or upset but we proved her wrong many times.

Through the years we have had many good times and many bad times. We've always worked as hard as we could to pay the bills and to provide for our family. From the beginning, many people told us we should not be together that the Big Guy was not good enough for me. Many thought our marriage would not make it. We've laughed together, cried together and bled together. Everything that we've been through has just brought us closer together. Things that have torn others apart have done the opposite for us.

At our 25th wedding anniversary, a friend asked me what the secret to a long happy marriage was. I wasn't sure how to answer because it took many things to come to where we were. All I can say is for a couple to stay together, they have to be meant to be together in the first place. You need to give true love in order to receive true love back. Honesty is very important and remember to keep the lines of communication open always. It takes work and sacrifice on both ends in order for it to work. Remember it is not always going to be easy but then again anything worthwhile is never easy.

Trust is another thing we share. The Big Guy knows what is in my heart and I know what is in his heart. No matter what anyone says or does, we have a very strong trust between us. I know he is a big flirt and loves to tease other women. He only teases our friends and they all know full and well where his heart lies. I know no matter what he says or does, it is I who holds the key to his heart.

The same goes for him. He is the sole owner of the key to my heart. This is a fact that has held true and strong throughout the years. I believe this bond of trust grows stronger with each passing day and is a huge reason why we've been able to weather any and all obstacles that have seemed to come our way. Without it, we would have been doomed from the beginning.

For all my years, I know I don't have the answers to every question and problem that arises. There is one thing that I do know. Remember I told you I figured out what true love is? Well, I will clue you in to what I found out. For love to make it and survive, it must be given as well as received. It has to be a two-way street. One cannot carry the load for two not when it comes to love. Imagine you are talking with the Good Lord and he asks you a question. He tells you he needs a life and you have a choice. Should he take your life or your lover's life? The answer must come quick as a heartbeat.

You answer with "Take mine!" because you know without your lover your life means nothing. This same question must be asked of your lover. The answer must be the same in return. If there is any hesitation or any time at all spent on thinking about the answer, the love between the two is not true love and it will not last the hardships of life. It may be crude, but it is the only way I found to tell the difference between love and lust. Think about it and you will find it is true.

I know now that everything we went through, all the hard times, all the good times it all points to life and the quality you make it. If you let things get you down, you will be down. If you smile and take things on the cuff and always remember that even though today may be bad, it doesn't mean tomorrow will be too because it is just another day to change things.

You never really know what a difference you make to folks unless you really look for it. Life is not a privilege; it is a gift and one we should never take for granted. Above all, life is really short and should never be wasted. Sometimes chances should be taken and roses need to be looked at and smelled because if you don't, you may find yourself old and alone and wondering where time went.

I for one do not want that to happen. I want to take time to smell the roses. I want to take chances. I want to try new things. I want to live. I am so glad I followed my heart all those years ago. I look back and sometimes marvel at all I have and all I know. I often wonder about where my life would have been, but then I know if I had listened, I would never have known the love and family I now love and cherish.

The story I started all those years ago does not end here. It goes on and on. Each day brings new air and new experiences. I wake up and greet each day knowing something new needs to be learned. One of the Big Guy's favorite sayings was if you don't learn something every day or make a mistake, then that means you've done nothing and haven't lived. One day I will tell you all about it in the next edition, Painted by Words, The Next Coat!

I thank God for all I have and know that I must continue down the path I have chosen. No matter what happens, no matter what I have to do or problem I have to solve, I won't be alone. I have my partner, my other half helping me do whatever it is and I am comforted and secure. For all in all, I know that I am truly blessed. I have the greatest gift of all. I have the gift of love.

Conclusion

In all my years of living, for all the trials, tribulations, for all the joy and heartache, for all my ups and downs, for all the laughs and tears I been through, I have decided on a few ideas. First of all, I have made a resolve to do the very best I can in whatever life decides to throw my way; to never give up or quit trying. Second, I resolve to treat each day as though it were the first and last, all mixed up into one. To never take for granted the simple pleasures and to always take time to give hugs and kisses and just say, "I love you." And lastly, I will see and treat myself as the person I know myself to be. The person that is inside and I truly know is there and I will definitely not see that person that other folks have tried so hard to create. That person does not exist, because it is not real. It has only been Painted by Words.

House on the Hill
Written by:
Mark J. Groom

Now I promise to you to build a house on the hill
Where the love that we have will keep us from all harm
And I promise to you our love will be as strong
As the house that I build on the hill
Well, our love will flow like the river in the valley below
And the skies up above where the cold wind blows
And my love for you will always be as strong
As the house that I build on the hill
Now the house that I build will keep us warm when it's cold,
Keep us dry when it rains Sheltered when the wind blows
And my love for you will always be as strong as
The house that I build on the hill
Now the house that I build; it will have a front porch
Where we'll sit side by side and grow old
And my love for you will always be as strong
As the house that I build on the hill

Printed by Libri Plureos GmbH in Hamburg, Germany